ENCOUNTERING JESUS, ENCOUNTERING SCRIPTURE

Encountering Jesus, Encountering Scripture

Reading the Bible Critically in Faith

David Crump

WILLIAM B. EERDMANS PUBLISHING COMPANY
GRAND RAPIDS, MICHIGAN / CAMBRIDGE, U.K.

Published 2013 by

Wm. B. Eerdmans Publishing Co.

2140 Oak Industrial Drive N.E., Grand Rapids, Michigan 49505 /

P.O. Box 163, Cambridge CB3 9PU U.K.

Printed in the United States of America

19 18 17 16 15 14 13   7 6 5 4 3 2 1

·   **Library of Congress Cataloging-in-Publication Data**

Crump, David, 1956-

Encountering Jesus, encountering scripture: reading the Bible critically in faith /

David Crump.

p.   cm.

Includes bibliographical references and index.

ISBN 978-0-8028-6466-6 (pbk.: alk. paper)

1. Bible. N.T. — Criticism, interpretation, etc.   2. Jesus Christ.

3. Kierkegaard, Søren, 1813-1855.   I. Title.

BS2361.3.C78   2013

225.6 — dc23

2012039339

www.eerdmans.com

Contents

Foreword

Encountering Jesus, Encountering Scripture is part bombshell, part pastoral epistle. Because I know David Crump (and I can hear his distinct voice on every page) I know that this is a book penned in love — which is exactly why he's willing to get in your face and not let you off the hook. In that sense, Crump's book is a lot like books written by Kierkegaard. You pick up a book that promises "edifying discourses," looking for a bit of devotional comfort, and soon realize that the author has something very different in mind. He's going to build you up by putting his thumb on the throat of your existence and not letting go until you appreciate what's at stake: your very soul. But then again, nobody promised they were *comforting* discourses.

Which is just to say that both Kierkegaard and Crump have a way of chopping a path through all the brush of hermeneutical debates and academic wrangling about historical criticism to remind us of a simple but still disconcerting truth: that the point of Scripture is to encounter Jesus.

You might be tempted to think this is obvious. Trust me: in many quarters it is not. In some places, the Bible simply functions as a bookend to uphold the status quo of American civil religion or whatever sort of domesticated spirituality passes for "Christianity." In a sense, that grotesque dinner table prayer in Will Ferrell's NASCAR parody, *Talladega Nights*, ends up functioning as a back-handed Kierkegaardian critique. While we all purport to be praying to Jesus the Christ, risen and ascended and seated at the right hand of the Father, instead we end up praying to whatever domesticated version of Jesus suits our tastes and preferences. So everyone around the table starts to share: "I like to picture Jesus as . . ." This is the preface to all of our idolatries. And it functions as a debilitating filter when we read the Bible. The Scriptures are no longer revelation; they are simply a mirror. Instead of encountering Jesus there, we simply see ourselves. This is what Kierkegaard liked to call "Christendom." And in his delicious Danish irony, Kierkegaard warns us: it's hard to read the Bible in Christendom.

In other quarters, the encounter with Jesus is buffered and deferred in the name of intellectual "rigor," theological enlightenment, and overcoming "naïve" faith. Too often, Crump points out, an "academic" approach to the Bible — whether "liberal" or "conservative" — ends up making the Bible something other than the means by which we are existentially encountered by Jesus. To approach the Bible in this way creates a blast wall that serves to protect us from the explosion of that encounter. And it's in this context that Crump is clear and straightforward about his project:

> [M]y goal in this book is to secure thorough integration of heart, mind, and soul by keeping first things first. In the realm of Christian understanding, the most fundamental questions do not concern historical evidence, archaeological data, literary genre, or any of the sundry matters usually tied to the rational explanation of empirical evidence. Rather, the basic issues in this arena are epistemological and spiritual: How can a person come to know God? (p. 5)

In other words, what's at stake here is *existential,* and not merely intellectual. It is simply — and yet terrifyingly — a matter of *faith.* This doesn't make it anti-intellectual; rather, as Crump emphasizes, it is a matter of intellectual *passion* or what Kierkegaard calls "subjective" thinking. Such thinking is not characterized by the safe, cool distance of reflection but rather the existential heat of encounter.

This is why Kierkegaard says that any follower of Jesus — and hence any true reader of the Scriptures — is really a "contemporary" of Jesus. In Crump's words:

> Such contemporaneity makes the believing individual obediently available to Christ. Knowledge and research alone can never accomplish this. I may investigate the minutiae of peasant life in first-century Palestine, learn Aramaic, and memorize the ancient texts, but none of this will make me Jesus' contemporary. But if I make

myself obediently available to the presence of Christ in my life, that *will* make me his contemporary. (p. 76)

In this sense, I think one can situate *Encountering Scripture, Encountering Jesus* within a wider discussion about the theological interpretation of Scripture, associated with scholars such as Richard Hays, Joel Green, Kevin Vanhoozer, Todd Billings, and many others. Markus Bockmuehl, a leading articulator of theological interpretation, puts this in a Kierkegaardian vein: "The implied interpreter of the Christian Scripture is a *disciple*."[1] That this would be a radical assumption to float at the Society for Biblical Literature will give you a sense of the stream that Crump is swimming against in this important little book. Some might try to domesticate or blunt this argument by categorizing it as "conservative," and therefore something that they, as Enlightened and progressive, can condescendingly ignore. But this isn't conservative; this call is radical. It gets to the roots.

So this book is a return to first things. You might also think of it as a return to a first love (Rev. 2:4). At the heart of this book is David's testimony. When he appeals to the primacy of encountering Jesus in Scripture — reminding us of what should seem obvious — he does so as one who has spent time in the arid wilderness of a merely academic approach to the Bible. Again following Kierkegaard, Crump doesn't see faith as antithetical to doubt; it is only antithetical to *offense*. To submit oneself to the encounter with Jesus is not to arrive at some iron-clad certainty that solves all of your problems. You don't have to set aside your questions. You only have to stop letting those questions be a defense, an excuse to not take the leap. Because sometimes we want answers to those questions precisely to avoid encountering the Jesus who would rock our world.

This is why *Encountering Scripture, Encountering Jesus* raises fundamental questions about the relationship between the academic study of Scripture and Christian faith. Even more broadly, I think it raises foundational questions about the relationship between Christian scholarship and faith in Jesus.[2] At some point, reflection reaches the edge of that chasm

1. Markus Bockmuehl, *Seeing the Word: Refocusing New Testament Study* (Grand Rapids: Baker Academic, 2006) 92.

2. As such, this book is liable to fall between the cracks of our disciplinary silos and into the enduring gap between the academy and the church. And yet this very liability is why this book is so needed. Hence I'm writing this Foreword: in hopes of catching your attention before you dismiss it as not within your purview.

Kierkegaard discusses. And at that point, the question isn't whether the Gospel is believ*able,* but whether *you* will believe it. This is not an intellectual dodge; it is owning up to the scandal that is the message of the cross, which is foolishness to the purveyors of Reason (1 Cor. 1:18-31). But as Crump rightly notes, "anyone who has surrendered their reason at the foot of the cross will discover that Christ hands it back again to be used more appropriately and insightfully in the search for truth" (p. 112).

This is exactly why I hope and pray that *Encountering Scripture, Encountering Jesus* will be widely utilized as a small textbook to accompany courses in biblical studies at Christian colleges and seminaries. And if it's not inappropriate to say so, here's the strongest commendation I can give: this is a book I'd want my children to read. My children are now students at those Christian universities I have in mind, and I can imagine them in those courses. And I would be grateful if they had the opportunity and occasion to encounter the argument of this book. Not in order to make biblical studies "safe." Far from it. (Indeed, do we really expect a "safe" Christianity from Kierkegaard?) No, students and other interpreters need to read this book to be reminded that what's at stake in biblical studies is an encounter with the Lover of our souls. What will you choose?

JAMES K. A. SMITH

Acknowledgments

No author gives birth to literary progeny solo. Numerous conversations with friends, family, and colleagues have seasoned the ingredients that have gone into the creation of this particular offspring.

I am especially grateful to my wife, Terry, who always serves as the first line of editorial comment on everything I write. It doesn't hurt that she, too, has now become an avid Kierkegaard reader.

Special thanks are due to C. Stephen Evans, Suzanne McDonald, C. Michael Robbins, Jamie K. A. Smith, and Richard Whitekettle, who have each read parts or all of the manuscript and offered helpful suggestions at various stages of its completion.

Many thanks are due to the editorial work of Michael Thomson and John Simpson of Eerdmans Publishing. Their work has made the book far more readable than it would otherwise have been.

I also want to recognize the generous assistance provided by the administration and the Board of Trustees at Calvin College, who approved both a Calvin Research Fellowship (2008-2009) and a sabbatical (2010-2011), which allowed me to accomplish a great deal of research.

CHAPTER 1

Introduction

Try as I might, stewing over my questions in the seminary library while reading the Gospel of Luke was not producing any ready answers, which only caused my stewing to become more fervent. In the course of my studies, I had slowly become convinced that my teachers were right — in composing their books the four Evangelists (the Gospel-writers) had shaped and edited their sources. They were not only preservers but also interpreters of the traditions about Jesus.

Though this reads like old news to me these days, it was a new and disconcerting thought at that point in my life. It certainly was very different from what I had been taught to believe (at least implicitly) while growing up in the church — that the four Gospels offered fairly straightforward transcriptions of Jesus' words and deeds. If I allowed myself to accept this new idea that Matthew, Mark, Luke, and John had painted portraits of Jesus — the first-century man I believed was crucified, resurrected, and ascended into heaven — with no intention of rendering him precisely as he was, then where could I go to meet the real Jesus, *as he truly is* without a third party's interpretation getting in the way?

The various historical reconstructions offered by form-critics[1] and other scholars, including those who had launched what is sometimes called the second quest for the historical Jesus,[2] had not convinced me that

---

1. Form Criticism is a method of biblical criticism or interpretation that classifies sections of Scripture by their literary patterns and seeks to determine the original forms and historical contexts of those literary traditions.

2. This effort was an attempt to use historical rather than faith-based methods to con-

they offered any viable alternatives. Albert Schweitzer's verdict on the first quest seemed as apt for all later critics as it was for the first: each new investigator repeated his predecessors' mistakes. Projecting his own preconceived ideas back into history, each of these writers constructed a new "historical Jesus" shaped by his own prejudices while boasting "of the skill with which [he found his] own thoughts again in the past!"[3]

I was already convinced that the critics who thought themselves better equipped than the ancients to recover the Jesus of history were fooling themselves. I was not willing to follow one pied piper after another with their alluring "assured results" of modern critical methods. But now I was left to wonder: were the Gospel authors any different? When I read the Gospel of Mark, how certain could I be that the Jesus depicted there was indeed the man crucified at Calvary? Put another way, how much does the face of Jesus in Mark reflect the face of Mark the Evangelist? If that were not worrisome enough, many critics argued that the Gospel writers tailored their portraits of Jesus to fit the needs of the early church communities. What if the Jesus of Mark was nothing more than a ghost of Jesus meant to serve that rather anonymous and amorphous collective labeled the Markan community? Am I looking at Jesus of Nazareth, or am I seeing Mark wearing a Jesus carnival mask?

This was my dilemma.

I can't remember how long I actually sat at the table thinking and praying, waiting for some solution to appear. Eventually a light went on, and I will never forget that particular moment of crystalline clarity. It hit me like the proverbial ton of bricks. *If my Christian faith had led me to a true relationship with Jesus Christ, then the Christ I now know by faith is the true Jesus of history.*

Someone else may have found this solution totally unsatisfactory, but it stopped me dead in my meditative tracks. Whether it sounds provocative

---

struct a reliable biography of Jesus. The first such quest was identified by Albert Schweitzer and sought to separate "mythology" from the true Jesus of history. A second such "quest" was identified as beginning in the 1950s and sought to wrestle with the "constraints of history" as to what could and could not be fairly asserted about the historical Jesus. N. T. Wright and others have pointed to the current explosion of work on the question of the historical Jesus as yet a third quest prompted in part by a desire to understand Jesus more thoroughly within his first-century Jewish context.

3. *The Quest of the Historical Jesus* (ed. J. Bowden; trans. W. Montgomery, J. R. Coates, S. Cuppitt, and J. Bowden; Minneapolis: Fortress, 2001) 480.

and dangerous or strikes one as a superficial tautology, that moment has never left me. I believed then, and still believe today, that either the Jesus I know through my experience of faith is the resurrected Jesus of Nazareth, the Jesus of history, or my Christian faith is an illusion.[4] That epiphany left me with the firm belief that there are no other viable alternatives.

If my Christian faith was an illusion, then the real challenge I faced was not in learning to demythologize the New Testament, making it more rationally accessible, but in finding the courage to demythologize my entire lived experience of Christian faith and religion. Though undoubtedly some readers will accuse me of taking the coward's way out, I had seen and experienced far too much in my Christian faith that impressed me as genuine spiritual encounter. The option to jettison my 20-plus years of Christian life was a non-starter. Accepting the insights of redaction criticism[5] might prompt me to readjust particular articulations of my faith, or certain tenets, but it was not nearly convincing enough to deconstruct it altogether. From that moment on I have remained convinced that the centerpiece, the integrating point of my life with Christ, both devotional and intellectual, must be found in this experience of personal encounter forged in faith. Throughout seminary, doctoral studies, pastoral ministry, and college teaching, the conviction that my personal faith commitment leads me to experience the real Jesus has become the meeting ground for theological inquiry as well as for a deeper personal intimacy with the living Christ.

Though I would not come to realize it for another 25 years, this early conviction about the unavoidably experiential foundation of my knowledge about Jesus Christ — and thus the inherent subjectivity of my (indeed, everyone's) search for theological and spiritual understanding — was the beginning of a journey that would eventually lead me to the doorstep of a Danish thinker, an iconoclast named Søren Kierkegaard. Though he never dismissed the value of historical research altogether, Kierkegaard staunchly defended the same view that I had intuited: the true Jesus is met through faith — not through historical information no matter how precise and accurate. Though he presents this thesis in a multitude of ways throughout his writings, let me begin introducing you to Kierkegaard's thought using

---

4. Fans of Christopher Hitchens' virulent atheism should read the entire book before chanting, "I told you so."

5. Redaction criticism examines how an early biblical editor or "redactor" might have shaped and molded the narrative to express a particular set of theological or other goals.

an example from one of his explicitly religious meditations, something he called an "edifying (or upbuilding) discourse." Kierkegaard insists that:

> We sometimes speak of learning to know God from the history of past ages; we take out the chronicles and read and read. Well, that may be all right . . . but how dubious the outcome frequently is. . . . But someone who is conscious that he [or she] is capable of nothing at all has every day and every moment the desired and irrefragable opportunity *to experience* that God lives.[6]

In other words, historical research can be useful, but it may obscure as easily as it illuminates since the historian is no less subject to personal bias than were the most conscientious Gospel authors and their attentive readers. The key, therefore, to real encounter with Jesus is not a more precise reconstruction of the past but a very contemporary step of faith realized in a profound awareness of personal need. This honest admission of individual helplessness and utter dependence before God Kierkegaard refers to as "the Moment." Such is the stuff that propels the initial and ongoing steps of faith. Life is an ongoing series of such "Moments," in which we confront the decision of faith over and over again: Will I entrust myself entirely to Jesus Christ, acknowledging that I am completely dependent on him for direction in this life as well as my hope in the next?

This pathway of faith is not just one possibility among many. It is not an anti-intellectual evasion of difficult questions or a mystical mantra circumventing reason or analysis. It is not a pietistic ruse for ceding history's *terra firma* to the barbarian hordes of critics, skeptics, and sundry university professors of religion. Neither does it have anything to do with the peculiar nature of the Gospels, their methods of composition, or doubts about their historical reliability. It is quite simply the only avenue available for authentic Christian understanding, given the distinctive natures of both the seeker (self-deceived sinners like us) and the Sought (an incarnate, resurrected Savior). Only taking the step of faith can bridge the vast, essential chasm (what Kierkegaard calls the "infinite qualitative difference") gaping wide between two such disparate characters as the Savior and the saved.

---

6. "To Need God Is a Human Being's Highest Perfection," in *Eighteen Upbuilding Discourses* (ed. and trans. Howard V. and Edna H. Hong; Princeton: Princeton University Press, 1990) 322, emphasis added.

In confessing my personal and academic affinity for Kierkegaard and his understanding of faith, I speak as a biblical studies professor who is regularly confronted with the naïve if heartfelt piety of students in North America. Bewildered by the amount of ancient history I expect them to learn, and often assuming they "know" all they need to know already, they may complain:

Why do I need to know this stuff?
What does that have to do with Bible study?

I cannot help but admonish such students with wrinkled brows and glassy eyes that they are uniquely privileged to have access to the world of the Bible, that their higher education is a gift and not a curse. Though I insist on the priority of personal faith and religious commitment in knowing Jesus, this is in no way intended to excuse anyone from the hard work and rewards of learning. I do not intend to segregate heart from mind, nor devotion from education. On the contrary, my goal in this book is to secure thorough integration of heart, mind, and soul by keeping first things first. In the realm of Christian understanding, the most fundamental questions do not concern historical evidence, archaeological data, literary genre, or any of the sundry matters usually tied to the rational explanation of empirical evidence. Rather, the basic issues in this arena are epistemological and spiritual: How can a person come to know God?

When it comes to the more basic problem of *precisely how* a person enters into an authentic understanding of God Almighty, discussion of evidence, arguments, science, and conclusions — no matter how careful — only amount to "sound and fury, signifying nothing."[7] The beginning of that I-Thou encounter with God is the launch into the spiritual universe that surrounds us. If that foundation is askew, we will not be able to achieve balance between mind and heart, evidence and faith, will and emotion. Without this foundation we begin our spiritual journey from the wrong place, and, though it is possible to redirect once we find our bearings, such corrections are difficult and slow. If you will allow me to change metaphors again, the religious life with its theological underpinnings behaves more like an oil tanker than a hovercraft: you can change courses, but it involves time and calculation as it requires a sizeable amount of self-

7. *Macbeth* V.5.

conscious effort. It is far better to begin correctly. Even though the old adage exclaims "All's well that ends well," in the realm of the religious life it is even truer to insist that all's well that begins well. Good beginnings are more important than good endings, since a misbegotten start can leave one lost or collapsed from wasted effort.

Much of the discussion about finding balance between intellect/education and piety/devotion is marred because extremists on both ends of the spectrum will use wedge issues to further the distance from those with opposing views. Those whose faith is more emotion-based sometimes seem to promote a grotesque brand of anti-intellectualism. A pastor once told me that the intellect must be abandoned in order to make room for faith. Most of us have encountered such an extreme point of view from time to time. Meanwhile, professors of theology sometimes behave as if the reified air of objectification and disinterested research should be the standard atmosphere for everyone in the church. Most of us have met professors who can cynically and unself-consciously dismiss the religious enthusiasm of students and others. Those who denigrate their opponents on the other end of this spectrum tar themselves with the same brush. Each extreme in this debate is actually a mirror image, the shadow self, of the other. Each represents a half of the creature *homo religiosus,* and each in some way needs the other to be complete.

A Personal Journey

It was while I wrestled with these questions during my years in seminary that I wandered into Kierkegaard's neighborhood. Even so, it took several decades before I arrived at his front door to read his work for myself. Actually, this intellectual journey did not begin with this famous Dane. My initial exposure to this point of view came by way of a famous German New Testament theologian, Rudolf Bultmann — the very one I had once been warned to avoid at all cost.

While I was preparing a paper on the prologue to John's Gospel, my research led me to Bultmann's important commentary.[8] It was hardly the first commentary I had ever read. My library contained quite a few. Still, I

---

8. *The Gospel of John: A Commentary* (trans. G. R. Beasley-Murray, R. W. N. Hoare, and F. K. Riches; Philadelphia: Westminster, 1971).

had never before read a commentary quite like this one. Woven in between the footnotes and excursuses on Greek word usage, Jewish theology, and Gnostic redeemer myths[9] was a clear exposition of how personal allegiance to Christ was the prerequisite for any accurate understanding of Christ's identity. Complete commitment, a radical surrender of personal allegiance, like a stomach-churning leap into the great unknown — this and only this would serve as the launching pad for genuine theological understanding of Jesus.

Though the existential fabric of Bultmann's thought may sound passé to twenty-first-century postmodern ears, it was all resoundingly new to me at the time. Bultmann convinced me not only of the theological-existential point that commitment precedes insight, but he argued persuasively that this was John's teaching, not his own invention. I found myself closing the book and pausing in order to absorb the weighty existential challenge Bultmann was pounding into me sentence after demanding sentence. Frankly, I had never before read a commentary, certainly not such an academic commentary, that assaulted both my mind and my will with claims that had immediate personal relevance. The analysis consistently forced itself on both my will and my heart. Here was a scholar (a German university professor no less!) telling me not only that Jesus Christ demanded my personal allegiance — a commitment that would completely reorganize my life and all of its priorities — but that I could never hope to grasp either the meaning of Jesus' historical identity or the significance of the New Testament message unless I first took this step of personal commitment.

I was taken completely by surprise. Unfortunately, I came to understand that what Bultmann intended to say was very different from what I initially took him to mean. Bultmann conceives of the object of faith in ways that I cannot accept.[10] But then, as I explored his understanding of the dynamics of faith, I encountered a scholar who refused to drive any wedges between faith and understanding, living and believing. I found in Bultmann a voice that went so far as to insist that authentic understanding, and thus authentic Christian living, can only arise from the personal

9. In Bultmann, the Christ "myth" in the New Testament is one variety of the Gnostic myth of the heavenly Redeemer. Its precursors are found in Iranian myths. In the New Testament version the dying and rising Savior is worked into the Christ figure and identified with a historical figure, Jesus of Nazareth.

10. See n. 17 below.

commitment that is faith. In describing the centrality of the incarnation, "the Word become flesh" in John 1:14, Bultmann explains that Christ

> . . . does not bring a teaching which renders his own presence superfluous; rather *as* the Incarnate he sets each [person] before the decisive question whether he [or she] will accept or reject *him*. So too the Gospel presents us with the peculiar dilemma, that it does not offer a real "teaching" of Jesus. . . . [T]o encounter the Revealer is not to be presented with a persuasive set of answers but only to be faced with a question. . . .
>
> The vision of faith takes place in the process of the upturning of all [human] natural aims in life. . . . This "seeing" is neither sensory nor spiritual, but it is the sight of *faith*. What faith sees . . . has never been perceived as an empirical event by anyone . . . it is not the contemplation of a timeless eternal truth but of the Word made flesh.[11]

Arriving at faith in the Word incarnate is not the inevitable result of a logical syllogism and doesn't follow as the obvious sum of a line of convincing evidence. It is always a step, perhaps even a leap, across an otherwise unbridgeable gap. Faith is the illuminating upward spark, struck from the friction of a one-to-one encounter between the willing individual and the man named Jesus of Nazareth. In that moment of friction a question arises: Will I entrust myself to this Jesus, the Word made flesh, the Redeemer now confronting me, challenging me in the gospel? Will I surrender to him as my Savior despite the fact that I may well still wrestle with unanswered questions? Will I do so even when the seemingly reasonable questions are of the sort that seems to insist on being answered before an intellectually honest faith is possible?

The question of faith poses an inherent challenge that cannot be ignored. The intellectual penchant for holding the gospel to some minimal threshold of empirical certainty before taking any such step (much less a leap) of faith permanently postpones the one thing necessary to finding answers: faith itself! Just as Jesus' teaching never "renders his own presence superfluous," neither is there any historical evidence or any rational argument that can substitute for the knowledge acquired through faith alone. This is always "the one thing lacking" (Mark 10:21).

11. *The Gospel of John*, 66, 70.

There are certain signs only faith can read, certain data only faith can take in. This apparent illogical dilemma is what qualifies faith *as faith*. As such, it is not a hypothesis, a theory, a conclusion, or something other than what it is. The offense of this dilemma is as unavoidable as it is immovable. I must be apprehended by Christ before I may hope to apprehend. This offensiveness is what Kierkegaard famously identified as the Paradox[12] or the Absurd,[13] that is, the inevitable enigma that must be fully embraced by all who wish to call themselves Christian.

One of Bultmann's favorite analogies, which perfectly captures Kierkegaard's own interest in the essentially personal and experiential nature of spiritual truth, explores the character of friendship. Bultmann asks what distinguishes a person with friends from a person who has none. The difference is not necessarily that the first knows more about friendship than the second. In fact, a friendless person may actually be better equipped to describe true friendship in all its beauty. Such a person's observations and analyses of intimacy, personal boundaries, expectations, compatibility, reciprocity, and every other intricate dimension of friendship may be second to none. However, we all understand that such knowledge itself is no substitute for actually having and being a friend. Now, imagine that the friendless expert were suddenly to gain a real friend. What new knowledge would he or she acquire about friendship? Nothing in principle, but everything in particular. Knowing about friendship is qualitatively different from having a friend and thus becoming a friend to another. The expert's head knowledge about friendship may not change at all in principle, except that now each point may be illustrated with a story drawn from experience. Further, each story unveils how the one befriended is now being transformed. As Bultmann explains:

> In knowing my friend in the *event* of friendship, the events of my life become new — "new" in a sense that is valid only for me and visible only to me. . . . However well I can know in advance and in general what a friend is, and also know that friendship must surely

---

12. In works published under his own name such as *Practice in Christianity.*

13. He used the language of "the Absurd" under one of his various pseudonyms. A. McKinnon, "Søren Kierkegaard," in *Nineteenth Century Religious Thought in the West*, vol. 1 (ed. N. Smart, J. Clayton, S. Katz, and P. Sherry; Cambridge: Cambridge University Press, 1985) 181-214 catalogues the evidence and explains why only the pseudonymous writings ever refer to Christianity as "the absurd."

make my life new, the one thing I can never know in advance and in general is what my friend is to me.[14]

In describing the transformational quality of friendship, Bultmann is channeling Kierkegaard.[15] Both habitually insist that all genuine knowledge of Christ is utterly subjective. Neither deny the historical reality of Jesus. Both insist that the truth of the gospel is only grasped *as truth* once we abandon the offense of faith's offensiveness and take the obligatory leap of trusting Christ with our daily lives — moment by momentous moment. In receiving Christ's offer of friendship, I am transformed by faith into Christ's friend. Through this faith relationship the day-to-day events of my life become new in ways that I and I alone can understand because I and I alone experience them as transformed by the Savior, my friend.

What a blast of fresh air these existential proclamations were for me as a young seminary student! How often does the hard work of academic biblical and theological study infuse life with the ultimate personal demand? "Demand," not merely devotional sprinklings so easily added piecemeal to the beginning and end of a lecture. "Demand," not just homiletical sidebars highlighting how the real significance of a text is found in the way "it can preach." In reading Bultmann I heard the voice of a scholar who refused to separate knowledge from commitment, intellect from will, understanding from passion. And in learning from Bultmann I was being introduced to Søren Kierkegaard and to the reality of true faith.

Recovering a Lost Voice

Bultmann eventually recedes like a ghost in late twentieth- and early twenty-first-century biblical studies. By the dawn of the new millennium, Bultmann had been transformed from a scholar everyone must read into one hardly anyone reads.[16] While his work once dominated multiple as-

---

14. "The Historicity of Man and Faith," in *Existence and Faith: Shorter Writings of Rudolf Bultmann* (trans. Schubert M. Ogden; New York: Meridian, 1960) 100.

15. For the purposes of this study, Bultmann's engagement with the philosophy of Martin Heidegger and Heidegger's dependence on Kierkegaard do not need to detain us; see M. Wyschogrod, *Kierkegaard and Heidegger: The Ontology of Existence* (New York: Humanities, 1954).

16. K. Hamman, *Rudolf Bultmann: Eine Biographie* (Tübingen: Mohr, 2009).

pects of twentieth-century biblical studies, hermeneutics, and theology, casting an inescapable shadow until his death in 1976, his influence slowly and quietly dissipated like the mighty Colorado, a river that scours the Grand Canyon in Arizona but vanishes to barely a trickle by the time it reaches Mexico's desert sands.

I expect Bultmann's critics, especially certain theological conservatives, will have guffawed loudly by this point in my review. Most such critics are all too happy that the man from Marburg's influence is as extinct as the dodo. While I agree heartily with those who argue that certain components of Bultmann's program deserved to be abandoned,[17] I remain convinced that the existential core of Bultmann's theology — a core tracing its lineage back directly to Kierkegaard — comprises a precious theological baby tragically thrown out with the turgid critical bathwater. Bultmann's *and* Kierkegaard's way of seeing offers an indispensable guide into the New Testament language of faith and discipleship that can be especially valuable to biblical theology in a postmodern world.

Kierkegaard would not have any sympathy for either Bultmann's historical-critical methods or his anti-supernaturalism. Rather, Kierkegaard resoundingly condemns all "assistant professors" (as he mockingly refers to them) who depend on skeptical methods and their inevitably faithless assumptions. Unlike Bultmann, Kierkegaard insists that belief in the gospel miracles, especially the supernatural events of Jesus' incarnation, bodily resurrection, and ascension, is essential for any faith claiming to be Christian. However, both of these Lutheran churchmen peeled back the layers to the essential nature of New Testament faith, and the consequences of their thought deserve to be wrestled with afresh.

Kierkegaard and Bultmann still pose a stiff challenge to students of the Bible. They give a serious call to personally integrate theological understanding and existential commitment. Both remind us that the one living Christ stands at the center of all aspects of Christian existence, holding them together as a unitary, passionate enterprise. Indeed, when taken seriously, faith is *the* enterprise that determines the entirety of one's life in all its dimensions. Isolating any aspect of that enterprise from faith becomes a liv-

---

17. Such as his allegiance to the reductionist principles of historical criticism, an inadequate understanding of first-century Judaism, a cut-and-paste construction of a nonexistent Gnostic redeemer myth, highly subjective use of form criticism to adjudicate the authenticity of Jesus' sayings, and the tenuous connection allowed between the historical Jesus and the Christ of faith.

ing death. Separating lived experience from the demands of faith will drain life of its significance, leaving only an empty shell devoid of any substance.

Faith as the Product of Personal Encounter

In this book I explore the New Testament's portrayal of the paradox of faith as both the catalyst for and the consequence of a personal encounter with the living Christ — an encounter that begs recognition in every area of a believer's life. I do this in such a way as to demonstrate Kierkegaard's insights into the nature of faith and personal decision. This book is not an exercise in philosophical theology but rather a living New Testament theology.

New Testament theology as expressed here will help students of the Bible and theology who find themselves facing the not uncommon challenge of sustaining a lively faith in a very personal Savior while laboring in the academic vineyards. I well remember being a student and facing "crises" of faith in my own life during graduate school. Thankfully, I managed to hammer out sufficiently satisfying answers to my questions so that I could persevere in both my studies and my faith with conscience intact. But others have not fared so well.

I have known a few who dropped out of school not because of financial hardship but because they feared that the constant academic rigor was steadily strangling their spiritual core. They did not know how a healthy heart could coexist with an inquisitive, disciplined mind, or thought it impossible. A few others slowly but surely drifted away from their faith in Jesus altogether because they could never realize the personal, intellectual, and spiritual integration they needed to persevere. Once faith loses its power to make personal demands, to reorient life, or to generate personal transformation, it appears unreal, an imposter, a falsehood. When a "believing" individual faces this kind of unreality, activities such as biblical and theological studies may survive as career options, matters of professional standing and technical expertise, but they are no longer demonstrations of faithful, authentic Christian living. In such a case, the student who admits his or her loss and turns to other pursuits is perhaps the more honest traveler.

It is no accident that in some strains of American Christianity preachers not only joke about confusing the words *seminary* and *cemetery* but can count on a boisterous laughter or smiling approval from their congregations. Certainly, a pernicious anti-intellectualism shapes the mind of this part of the religious subculture, but it is not the whole story. Many devoted men and women in our colleges, seminaries, and graduate schools find themselves wrestling, sometimes with fear and trembling, over the personal integration of their formerly youthful faith and the sometimes threatening demands of higher learning. I hope and pray that this book may be of some help to those who struggle.

Defining Three Important Words

No one likes jargon. There may be authors hesitant to clarify what is more conveniently left obscure.[18] Imprecision only makes for misunderstanding and allows mental laziness to parade as profundity. So I should define now three terms that will loom large in everything that follows: faith, experience, and existential.

Faith is a personal decision to orient one's life to trust of and obedience to Jesus Christ. I will place particular emphasis on the subjective nature of Christian faith. With "subjective" I mean to highlight two qualities. First, Christian faith is never a deduction from logical argument alone. In this sense it is never "objective" because it is not established by reason alone. Reason is not excluded, but faith is never to be confused with mere intellectual assent, as if believing in Jesus were synonymous with believing in his teachings or his historical existence. Consequently, faith is not to be confused with doctrine or any other objectifiable "content."

The second quality of this subjectivity follows from the first. Christian faith requires the believer to enter a new realm of life that will never be completely grasped rationally. This is why some have referred to faith as a "leap." Whether or not it is a leap *in the dark* will be explored as this book unfolds. I argue that it is not, but readers must reach their own conclusions, since faith must be personal. The point here is not that a believer plunges into irrationality. Sometimes those who lack faith may see it that way. The point is rather that there is no predictable, inescapable line of progress from (a) studying Christianity or learning about the life of Jesus

---

18. For a skewering of philosophical jargon, especially among existentialists, see T. W. Adorno, *The Jargon of Authenticity* (trans. D. Tarnowski and F. Will; Evanston: Northwestern University Press, 1973).

to (b) actually entrusting one's life to Jesus Christ himself. That conclusive step of personal engagement and surrender is always discontinuous with everything that has ever gone before. Thus every step of faith is a subjective step of personal commitment.

Experience will be used here as a specifically relational term, referring to the subjective engagement and interaction that occurs in personal relationship. Such experience should not be confused with emotions, feelings, or fluctuations in sentiment. By Christian experience I mean the one-on-one relationship between the individual believer and the living Jesus himself. It is through such personal experience that the truth of Christ is shown to be true *for me.* There is a profound difference between announcing that Jesus is the truth for the world and experiencing by faith that Jesus is the truth for my life. Such experience is the necessary demonstration that I am actually living in the truth that I espouse. Just as no one else can exercise faith for me, so no one else can experience Christ for me. Authentic experience can only be one's own, and without it there is no true evidence of genuine faith. There are no particular, predetermined sensory requirements for such Christian experience, no predictable one-size-fits-all observable criteria. What matters is not what anyone else may observe or what the one having the experience may think he or she feels. All that matters is that the individual experiencing the experience knows by faith, however that conviction is secured, that the experience is an encounter with the resurrected Jesus. Since demonstrating that conclusion empirically is impossible, the Christian lives by faith.

Existential describes a life whose meaning and purpose is defined by owning the results of one's decisions in thought, word, and deed. External factors such as history, community, culture, and family may determine the environmental factors that influence our choices, but ultimately every individual must stand alone before God to give an account of the sum total of his or her personal decisions. There is no room for transferring the responsibility of those choices to others. Judgment of those consequences and our responsibility for each of them is God's prerogative, and divine judgment is inevitable. Understanding the eternal significance of individual responsibility and therefore choosing daily, moment by moment, to trust in and to obey Jesus Christ in our decisions is the substance of a truly Christian journey through life. When this is finally understood, it also becomes clear that Christian theology and ethics, as well as the more loosely defined areas of life such as piety and devotion, are all thoroughly existential endeavors.

CHAPTER 2

Recognizing the Messiah When You See Him

If the delusion under which Christendom has labored these many years were indeed true, that it was in fact directly visible that Christ was the one he claimed to be, then why such a strange response?

Anti-Climacus/Kierkegaard, *Practice in Christianity*

The earliest Christians insisted that their faith in Jesus Christ was rooted in the witness of the Old Testament. Paul tells the Corinthian church that he taught them what he himself had received: "that Christ died for our sins according to the Scriptures, and that he was buried, and that he was raised the third day according to the Scriptures" (1 Cor. 15:3-4). Not once but twice Paul insists that the message he preached conformed to an ancient narrative embedded within the holy writings of the people of Israel — it all happened *according to the Scriptures.* Scriptural warrant for the message about Jesus of Nazareth — now the risen Christ — has always been an essential ingredient of Christianity's truth claims. The Old Testament was foundational to the New Testament's argument that the church is the fulfillment of the Old Testament's expectations. Jesus is identifiable as Israel's long-awaited Messiah, foretold by the Law, the Prophets, and the Writings, because the Old Testament describes what it means for Christ to be Christ.[1]

---

1. The Law (Torah), the Prophets (Nebi'im), and the Writings (Ketubim) are the three divisions of Hebrew Scripture, often designated by the acronym "Tanakh." The New Testament claims that all three divisions contain promises fulfilled by Jesus.

Yet, as emphatically as the earliest Christians insisted on this predictive connection between the Old and New Testaments, their opponents were equally earnest in denying them the validity of their argument. Notice that Paul does not specify which Scriptures indicated that the Christ would die for sin, be buried, and then rise the third day. Nor does Paul say how those crucial theological lessons were to be discovered in the texts. Christian claims that the New Testament church and its message about Jesus fulfilled the expectations of the Jewish Scriptures drew as many guffaws as ahas from ancient audiences. To many listeners, the Christian pathway from the Old Testament to Jesus of Nazareth was anything but self-evident. For instance, the second-century anti-Christian critic Celsus observed that the prophecies purportedly fulfilled by the man from Nazareth "could be applied to thousands of others far more plausibly than to Jesus."[2]

Even allowing for a bit of rhetorical flourish, Celsus clearly found Christian interpretation of the Old Testament wholly unconvincing. In fact, he judged the value of such arguments for Christian apologetics (defense of the faith) not merely flimsy but fanciful to the point of distraction. Since it is unlikely that this Gentile adherent of Platonic philosophy was speaking from observations he had made into Israel's holy books, Celsus was almost certainly repeating well-worn accusations sharpened by years of Jewish-Christian debate in local synagogues. And even though the Christian apologist Origen tried to answer his charges (this was the goal of his book *Contra Celsum*), Celsus's question of what constitutes plausible interpretation has never stopped haunting the way Christians read the Old Testament. In fact, some 1600 years later Kierkegaard offered a typically blunt summary of this very problem in his book *Practice in Christianity* when he remarked on "the delusion" that Jesus' true identity should have been "directly visible" to his contemporaries.[3] On the contrary, nothing is direct about Jesus' relationship to the Old Testament or to Jewish expectations of the Messiah. Kierkegaard is an insider and yet honest enough to question the Christian tradition for its stubborn refusal to admit the obvious. If Jesus' fulfillment of messianic expectations were truly straightforward, why did so many seem oblivious to that reality? Why was Jesus not more widely embraced, at least by those most knowledgeable of the Scriptures? Even John the Baptist confessed his confusion over what to make of the man from Nazareth (Matt. 11:1-6). Celsus's cri-

---

2. *Contra Celsum* 2.28.
3. (Princeton: Princeton University Press, 1991), 95.

tique carries a lot of weight. He would probably have been more responsive to late afternoon conversations with an empathetic conversation partner like Kierkegaard than he was to Origen's forceful rhetoric.

A brief example will help to illustrate both Celsus's complaint and Kierkegaard's admission. The Gospel of Matthew contains a series of fulfill-ment quotations in which texts from the Old Testament are described as prophecies that have finally been "fulfilled" in the life and ministry of Jesus. Matthew 2:14-15 finds one such prophecy in Hosea 11:1, "Out of Egypt I called my son" (NIV). In its original context, Yahweh speaks through the pre-exilic prophet, contrasting Israel's past experience of divine mercy with the nation's ongoing disobedience. God recalls how he graciously chose the infant nation to become his son, rescuing its people from Egyptian slavery (see Exod. 4:22-23). Yet, rather than recall the exodus with gratitude and covenant faithfulness, Israel had chosen idolatry. God laments, "The more I called Israel, the further they went from me" (Hos. 11:2). Consequently he warns that, unless Israel repents, its people will be punished and "will re-turn to Egypt," this time because of Assyrian conquest and exile (Hos. 11:5).

Looking at what Matthew has done with this passage leaves one scratching one's head. First, it should be noted that Hosea 11:1 is not a pre-diction waiting to be fulfilled. It is a historical reminiscence used to high-light the divine justice of Israel's eventual conquest by the Assyrians in 722 B.C. There is no evidence that the text was ever read as a prophecy about the coming Messiah prior to its appearance in Matthew's Gospel. Hosea 11:1 "would not have been on anyone's list of 'obvious' messianic proof-texts."[4] Furthermore, not only does the content of Hosea 11:1 appear rather unserviceable to Matthew's apologetic purposes, but everything Matthew proceeds to do with Hosea is completely backward. For Hosea, Egypt was a place of oppression from which Israel needed to be rescued. For Matthew, Egypt was a place of refuge into which Jesus escaped the threats of King Herod. Certainly, Jesus must eventually "come out of Egypt" if he is ever to reside in Nazareth. However, if that was the connection motivating Mat-thew's use of the passage in Hosea, it seems strange for him not to have noted its fulfillment in connection with Matthew 2:20-21, when Jesus actu-ally leaves Egypt and returns to Israel. What possible reason does Matthew have for claiming that this particular story from the infancy narratives "fulfills" the words of Hosea 11:1? Even a scholar as guarded as C. F. D.

---

4. R. T. France, *The Gospel of Matthew* (Grand Rapids: Eerdmans, 2007) 12.

Moule describes Matthew's use of Hosea as "manifestly forced and artificial and unconvincing."[5]

Matthew's argument is less than persuasive, and it is highly unlikely that many synagogue members were convinced by such readings of the Old Testament. But Matthew was obviously convinced of the legitimacy of the fulfillment he was asserting. Likewise, his earliest readers and much of the ancient church followed suit as his became the most widely disseminated of the four Gospels. For those ancient first readers willing to entertain the possibility of sharing in Matthew's faith concerning Jesus Christ, the connections Matthew drew between Israel-as-son and Jesus-as-son became spiritually illuminating. They accepted the integrity of his interpretive strategy. Seeing Jesus as the true Israel is a major theme in Matthew's work. But it is only acceptable from a reading that is already sympathetic to Matthew's message.

It is precisely because of this sympathetic prerequisite that neither Celsus nor his skeptical comrades would ever be satisfied with Matthew's approach to scriptural argument. For the unsympathetic reader, it will always appear that Hosea 11:1 could be applied to others "far more plausibly than to Jesus." It is impossible to grasp Matthew's fulfillment arguments without first making some attempt at the willing suspension of disbelief. The persuasive power of the New Testament's use of the Old Testament in proof-texts relies on the reader's willingness to set aside seemingly reasonable objections and to exercise faith. As Kierkegaard insists, arguments from reason, no matter how reasonable, are never in and of themselves a sufficient cause either to take or to refuse the step of faith. True faith is not the product of biblical or rational argument; it is the first step in understanding and accepting such arguments. This certainly fits what we see in the way Matthew presents his case for Jesus. Without faith New Testament interpretation of the Old Testament makes little sense However, with faith new connections are forged. There emerges a way of seeing a relationship between the testaments that was never seen before. That is the way both revelation and faith work.

The wealth of literature in the field of intertextual biblical interpretation provides an embarrassment of riches for today's researcher.[6] Anyone

---

5. *The Origin of Christology* (Cambridge: Cambridge University Press, 1977) 129.

6. Intertextuality refers to the ways in which earlier texts are embedded within later texts, either explicitly or implicitly, by quotation or allusion, and the reciprocal influence each has on the other in the work of interpretation. For an introductory discussion, see R. Hays, *Echoes of Scripture in the Letters of Paul* (New Haven: Yale University Press, 1989) 14-21 and the bibliography in n. 50 on p. 198.

who plans to investigate how the New Testament writers interpret the Old Testament will benefit from having some guiding principles to help them navigate the sprawling literature at their disposal. Opening this chapter with the classic confrontation between Celsus and Origen gives us just such a guiding principle: the role of faith. Keeping in mind Kierkegaard's sympathy for the struggles of a man like Celsus and his dismissal of the forced interpretations left to the church by apologists like Origen underscores the importance of faith as a precursor to understanding. Kierkegaard went through years of theological training in preparation for the pastorate, but he seems to have embraced a more biblical way of seeing than some theologians and philosophers had. He was clearly well versed in Matthew and the rest of the Scriptures and shared the faith-based understanding of his biblical forbears. By examining the New Testament's use of the Old Testament we find a fascinating synergy with Kierkegaard's biblically formed understanding of *faith as a well-considered act of passionate commitment.*

The Messiah No One Expected

The blockbuster science fiction movie *The Matrix* depicts an intriguing vision of the future. The movie's hero, a computer hacker named Neo, finds his familiar, if seedy, life suddenly invaded by an apparently omniscient stranger named Morpheus. Morpheus offers Neo a little red pill that he promises will forever change the way Neo sees himself, his life, and his world. Swallowing the pill enables Neo to perceive reality for the very first time. What he learns is that everything he has ever experienced was literally all inside his head; his entire life was an illusion, a complicated computer simulation game running through his brain. He wakes up, his atrophied body floating in a cubicle filled with liquid nutrients, limbs plugged in to the all-controlling Matrix. He now recognizes that his life has never been what he thought it was because it was never anything more than the thoughts of what he thought he was. His life story as a scruffy computer hacker evaporates before his very eyes just as every illusion must, once confronted by the contradictions of reality.

Some of my readers may feel like they are being asked to take such a pill. The analogy may be apt because reality, however awkward, is always an improvement over illusion, even very comforting illusions. Understanding how and why the New Testament writers interpret the Old Testament as they do requires facing a profound historical reality: no one had ever expected a Messiah like Jesus.[7] His life and ministry were completely, totally, unmitigatedly, and unapologetically unanticipated by any of the biblical or extra-biblical traditions relating to Jewish messianic hopes. Some of the earliest Christians in the ancient church were willing to recognize the conundrum. By the early second century Ignatius of Antioch (ca. 50-117) referred to Christ as the hidden Word that was created in[8] and proceeded from[9] the shadows of heavenly silence[10] so that God might keep his plans hidden from Satan.[11] It was no accident that the Old Testament revealed nothing about the details of Christ's ministry: God had deliberately hidden his intentions so as not to tip his hand prematurely to the enemy.

The idea that Jesus somehow, consciously or unconsciously, followed a preexisting messianic paradigm, written or symbolic, that he healed the sick, raised the dead, forgave sins, was crucified, rose on the third day, and then ascended to heaven in conformity with detailed Old Testament prophecy and Jewish expectations is a grand *Matrix*-like illusion. Although most would reject the idea that Jesus was following a comprehensive messianic blueprint (who has never heard the claim that Jesus failed to fulfill traditional expectations?), still the illusion persists nevertheless in more subtle forms.

What were the messianic hopes of the Jews in the Judaism of Jesus' day (often called Second Temple Judaism)? How are these hopes and expectations related to the way we read and interpret the Bible and the relationship between Old and New Testament? There is a close relationship between these two questions. To answer one, we need to look at both. I will provide now a brief survey of the current consensus among historians of Second Temple Judaism. This will clarify the historical questions enough that we should be able to lay some foundation for the role of faith in understanding the New Testament's interpretation of the Old Testament.

---

7. Throughout this chapter I use the word *Messiah* as a general term for an agent of God's eschatological deliverance to Israel. It is not intended to prejudice how we might answer questions about the character of the agent(s), the nature of the future, or the kinds of actions that will bring deliverance.

8. *Ephesians* 19.1.

9. *Magnesians* 8.2.

10. *Hēsychia, sigēs.*

11. Cf. *Philadelphians* 8.2.

First, most scholars and students of the New Testament era recognize the extraordinary diversity of the messianic hopes that were circulating then. The bibliography on this question is so extensive that there is no good reason to recall all the evidence here.[12] A brief review is adequate for our purposes. If we put to one side that many Jews were not expecting any sort of Messiah-deliverer[13] and only consider those that did entertain such hopes, we find a wide variety of possible messianic figures from which to choose. The Messiah might be a king[14] (not necessarily in the Davidic line),[15] a prophet[16] (a new Moses or Elijah), a priestly representative,[17] or even an angelic figure from heaven such as Michael the archangel,[18] Melchizedek,[19] or someone "like the Son of Man."[20]

Second, in spite of this diversity, it is noteworthy that there was no ex-

---

12. See E. P. Sanders, *Judaism: Practice and Belief 63 BCE–66 CE* (Philadelphia: Trinity, 1992) 295-98. Sanders's summary is to the point: "[W]hen Jews who thought about the future concretely sat down to describe it, they did not have only one model to follow. They all trusted in God. *That* is common. There seems to have been no overwhelming consensus about what people he would use, and what their descent would be; and indeed some thought that he would do everything himself" (298). See also J. Neusner, W. S. Green, and E. Frerichs, eds., *Judaisms and Their Messiahs at the Turn of the Christian Era* (Cambridge: Cambridge University Press, 1987); J. J. Collins, *The Scepter and the Star: Messianism in Light of the Dead Sea Scrolls* (2d ed.; Grand Rapids: Eerdmans, 2010); N. T. Wright, *Jesus and the Victory of God* (Minneapolis: Fortress, 1996) 481-89; J. H. Charlesworth, H. Lichtenberger, and G. S. Oegema, eds., *Qumran-Messianism: Studies on the Messianic Expectations of the Dead Sea Scrolls* (Tübingen: Mohr, 1998); W. Horbury, *Jewish Messianism and the Cult of Christ* (London: SCM, 1998). For a handy summary of the evidence, see K. E. Pomykala, "Messianism," in *The Eerdmans Dictionary of Early Judaism* (ed. J. J. Collins and D. Harlow; Grand Rapids: Eerdmans, 2010) 938-42.

13. Sanders, *Judaism*, 295, goes so far as to say, "The expectation of a messiah was not the rule."

14. *Psalms of Solomon* 17; *4 Ezra* 11:1–12:3; 4Q252 V.1-4; 4QFlor I.10-13.

15. 1QS 9:10-11; CD 12:23; and 1QSa 2:20 refer to a Messiah of Israel. CD 7:19-20; 1QM 5:1-2; 1QSb 5:20-29; and 4Q285 describe one called the Prince of the Congregation. 4Q246 refers to the Messiah as Son of God and Son of the Most High. Whether any of these are Davidic figures is disputed. *Sibylline Oracles* 3.652-56 speaks of a king from the sun liberating Israel.

16. 4Q521; 1QS 9:11.

17. *Jubilees* 31:11-17; *Testament of Levi* 18:2-5; 1Q21 fragments 3 and 4; CD 7:18-20; 12:23–13:1; 14:19; 19:10-11; 20:1; 1QS 9:10-11; 1QSa 2:11-15; 4QFlor I.11-12.

18. 1QM 13:10; 17:7-8.

19. 11QMel.

20. *1 Enoch* 46:3-6; 48:2-6; *4 Ezra* 13.

pectation in any of the literature that the Messiah must die. You will find nothing about a death by crucifixion or any other means, or that the Messiah's death would have vicarious, atoning value. Furthermore, there was no expectation of his resurrection and exaltation.[21]

Third, the lack of a Jesus-like dying and rising Messiah in the Jewish literature of the time is not surprising once it is understood that there are no such examples in the Old Testament precedents. Even among the passages referred to by the Evangelists, either in connection with Jesus' teaching about his fate[22] or in the Passion (arrest, trial, and crucifixion) narratives,[23] we do not find any pre-Christian Jewish interpreters forecasting a dying and rising Messiah.[24]

Fourth, there is no reason to assume that resurrection and exaltation per se would have caused Jewish people at the time to understand any figure as Messiah. "There was no Jewish doctrine of the appointment of a Messiah . . . through the resurrection and exaltation of a dead man."[25]

Fifth, Deuteronomy 21:23 made it immensely difficult, if not impossi-

21. 4 *Ezra* 7:29-30 is the only extant text in which the Messiah dies. His death comes after a four-hundred-year reign, and no significance is attached to it: it does not accomplish anything. Eventually, the general resurrection occurs for everyone, but the Messiah is not singled out. The suggestion that Qumran expected a dying Messiah (4Q285) has been convincingly discredited; see M. Bockmuehl, "A 'Slain Messiah' in 4QSerekh Milhamah (4Q 285)?" *Tyndale Bulletin* 43 (1992): 155-69; J. H. Charlesworth and W. P. Weaver, eds., *The Dead Sea Scrolls and the Christian Faith* (Harrisburg: Trinity, 1998) 28-30. More recently, I. Knohl, *The Messiah before Jesus: The Suffering Servant of the Dead Sea Scrolls* (trans. D Maisel; Berkeley: University of California Press, 2000) has made the provocative suggestion that the Qumran community believed the historical Menahem, a contemporary of Hillel (referred to in Mishnah *Ḥagigah* 2:2), died as a suffering Messiah; however, see the convincing critiques of J. Collins in *Jewish Quarterly Review* 91 (2000): 185-90 and J. O'Neill in *Dead Sea Discoveries* 8 (2001): 315-18.

22. Such as Exod. 24:8, 11 in Matt. 26:28; the "sign of Jonah" in Matt. 12:39-41; 16:4; Luke 11:29-32; Ps. 118:22-23 in Mark 12:10-11 par. Matt. 21:42 par. Luke 20:17; Isa. 53:1 in John 12:38; Isa. 53:12 in Luke 22:37; Jer. 32:6-9 in Matt. 27:9; Zech. 9:9 in Matt. 21:4-5; John 12:15; Zech. 9:11 in Mark 14:24 par. Matt. 26:28; Zech. 11:12-13 in Matt. 27:10; Zech. 12:10 in John 19:37; Zech. 13:7 in Mark 14:27 par. Matt 26:31.

23. Such as Exod. 12:46 (or Num. 9:12; Ps. 34:20) in John 19:36; Ps. 22:1 in Mark 15:34 par. Matt. 27:46; Ps. 22:18 in John 19:24; Pss. 35:19; 69:4 in John 15:25; Ps. 41:9 in John 13:18; Zech. 12:10 in John 19:37.

24. D. Juel, *Messianic Exegesis: Christological Interpretation of the Old Testament in Early Christianity* (Philadelphia: Fortress, 1992) 8, 12-13, 89-117; Collins, *Scepter,* 123-26.

25. M. Hengel, *The Atonement: The Origins of the Doctrine in the New Testament* (trans. J. Bowden, Philadelphia: Fortress, 1981) 41.

ble, to consider someone who was crucified to be messianic.[26] This grue-some form of Roman execution would have been a repugnant fate for any supposed savior among Gentile audiences and would have ranked as blasphemy among Jews.[27] In the second-century treatise *Dialogue with Trypho,* Justin's Jewish antagonist Trypho objects to the message of a crucified Messiah by quoting Deuteronomy 21:23 and calling this idea "blasphemy," saying that "he who is crucified is to be accursed."[28]

Finally, there was no pre-Christian expectation of a messianic Suffering Servant modeled after Isaiah 52:13–53:12. Jewish interpretation of Isaiah did not link the Servant passages together as the depiction of a single individual. Coordination of the four so-called Servant Songs,[29] abstracted from their surrounding context in Isaiah 40–55, is a modern construction.[30] Although *Targum Jonathan*[31] provides a messianic interpretation of the Servant in Isaiah 53, the suffering in this passage is displaced onto the nation of Israel and its enemies. H. S. Levey concludes concerning the messianic thought of the targum that there is "no room whatsoever for a suffering and dying Messiah."[32] Frankly, this can be said of all Second Temple literature.[33]

---

26. Hengel, *Atonement,* 43-44.

27. M. Hengel, *Crucifixion in the Ancient World and the Folly of the Message of the Cross* (trans. J. Bowden; Philadelphia: Fortress, 1977).

28. *Dialogue* 32 and 89; *Dialogue with Trypho* is typically dated early in the second half of the second century A.D.

29. Isa. 42:1-4; 49:1-6; 50:4-9; 52:13–53:12.

30. For a good survey of the issues surrounding the New Testament appeal to the Isaianic servant, see Wright, *Jesus,* 588-92.

31. The targumim are Aramaic translations and exposition of the Hebrew Scriptures. They circulated in the synagogues of Second Temple Judaism once Hebrew had effectively become a dead language in post-exilic Israel. *Targum Jonathan* covers the prophets.

32. *The Messiah: An Aramaic Interpretation — The Messianic Exegesis of the Targum* (Cincinnati: Hebrew Union College Press, 1974) 67. It is impossible to know with any degree of certainty whether this section of the targum reflects pre- or post-Christian Palestinian tradition. It is equally baseless to characterize it as an anti-Christian polemic, despite the claims of J. Jeremias in *Theological Dictionary of the New Testament,* vol. 5 (ed. G. Friedrich; trans. G. Bromiley; Grand Rapids: Eerdmans, 1968) 692 n. 289, 695. Jeremias's arguments are ably addressed by J. Ådna, "The Servant of Isaiah 53 as Triumphant and Interceding Messiah: The Reception of Isaiah 52:13–53:12 in the Targum of Isaiah with Special Attention to the Concept of the Messiah," in *The Suffering Servant: Isaiah 53 in Jewish and Christian Sources* (ed. B. Janowski and P. Stuhlmacher; trans. D. P. Bailey; Grand Rapids: Eerdmans, 2004) 190-94.

33. Including later rabbinic traditions with pre-Christian roots. The teachings of the

It is crucial for readers of the New Testament today to understand that Jesus' followers had no mental framework in which to fit a humiliated, suffering, crucified, or resurrected Messiah.[34] His words were the equivalent of someone today predicting that next year's Indianapolis 500 will be won by a thoroughbred named Suffering Servant. Is it any wonder that the twelve disciples failed to understand what Jesus was saying about his call?

Coming to grips with why the New Testament interprets the Old Testament as it does must begin here. Readers must face up to the vast historical break between all known forms of pre-Christian messianic expectation and the confident apostolic claims of messianic fulfillment in Jesus of Nazareth. Those who approach the New Testament with long-term familiarity and have inherited a thoroughly Christian history of its interpretation are easily blinded from recognizing how unprecedented these connections between the testaments were. While we may take for granted connecting Jesus' arrest with the injured shepherd of Zechariah 13:7 (Matt. 26:31), Jesus' passion with the Suffering Servant in Isaiah 53 (1 Pet. 2:21-25), and the empty tomb with a Davidic hope for resurrection in Psalm 16:8-11 (Acts 2:25-28), all these readings would have caused Celsus to pull his hair out in bewildered protest. We must resist the temptation of allowing widely attested pre-Christian understandings of such Old Testament passages to fade away and disappear in the face of our great familiarity with New Testament uses of the same texts. Christian readings are

---

rabbis did not begin to be codified until the second half of the second century with the composition of the Mishnah. However, some of these rabbinic perspectives were certainly in circulation in the time of Jesus.

34. Regrettably, this historical information continues to be overlooked by the popularizers of evidential apologetics. For one particularly egregious example, see L. Strobel, *The Case for Faith: A Journalist Investigates the Toughest Objections to Christianity* (Grand Rapids: Zondervan, 2000) 266-67, who writes, "In effect, dozens of these Old Testament prophecies created a fingerprint that only the true Messiah could fit. This gave Israel a way to rule out imposters and validate the credentials of the authentic Messiah. Against astronomical odds . . . Jesus and only Jesus throughout history, matched this prophetic fingerprint." How unfortunate that the disciples never learned how to fingerprint their own Messiah. Apparently, the many devout men and women who suffered violent deaths at Roman hands while following one or another of the various alternative messiahs were equally misinformed about their own Scriptures; for a survey of how other Messiah-figures read the Old Testament and presented themselves as its fulfillment, see S. McKnight, *Jesus and His Death: Historiography, the Historical Jesus, and Atonement Theory* (Waco: Baylor University Press, 2005) 177-84.

more familiar to Christian readers, but in the history of interpretation they were the innovations.

Here, then, is the challenge: Jesus' disciples stood at the precipice of a vast historical chasm separating *all* Christian New Testament claims to fulfillment from *every* known Old Testament Jewish forbear. How was the disparity to be reconciled?

Perhaps God had decided to change the means of fulfilling those texts. If this were the case, one wonders what was the point of attending to the Scriptures if the Lord might freely depart from prior revelation and its apparent meaning at the very moment when it mattered most. What, then, was the point of messianic prophecy in the first place?

On the other hand, if the Lord had not changed plans but was still pursuing Scripture's original intentions, the question remains: What is the point of attending to Scripture if its fulfillment can be so radically unlike prediction that it becomes impossible to deduce the one from the other? Again, what was the point of prophecy?

Perhaps Ignatius was on to something. Does messianic interpretation bring us into an impenetrable realm of divine mystery? As we will see, a fundamental challenge for all New Testament interpretation involves a proper appreciation of the role of faith. The faith required to accept this messianic interpretation of Scripture is not the result of any conclusion derived from a prior understanding (such as "I believe this is fulfillment because I see its connection to the prediction"). Rather, New Testament faith is understood as a willingness to keep in step with *whatever* God may be doing *right now*, regardless of whether it was predicted, anticipated, foreseen, or understood in advance.

Crossing the Historical Chasm

The historical divide separating Old Testament anticipation from New Testament claims to fulfillment can be crossed in one way and one way only: by jumping. There are no interpretive bridges to transport a reader *from* the Old Testament antecedents *to* the New Testament insistence on fulfillment in Jesus Christ. All attempts to describe such historical-exegetical connections invariably show themselves to be sophisticated exercises in transposing New Testament theology back into the Old Testament texts while claiming to do the opposite. Such interpretive attempts invariably build their bridges *backward* — by presupposing Christian faith and looking for the Old Testament antecedents — while presenting themselves as historical-grammatical studies of Old Testament literature.[35] This must be recognized for the interpretive sleight of hand that it is. It is one thing to confess the existence of the theological presuppositions a reader brings to the text. It is quite another to systematically insert those presuppositions into the act of interpretation while claiming to demonstrate how those very beliefs are being derived from the text. Once a thoroughly Christian bridge is built from the New Testament back into the Old, an erudite theological conclusion is produced explaining how this is possible. Arguments supporting this shaky structure describe the Old Testament as filled with mystery, typology,[36] shadows, deeper meanings, organic links, creative developments, or something called *sensus plenior* (a "fuller sense"). This weighty vocabulary is waved about like a magic wand and *voila,* the newly discovered bridge crosses the canonical divide. At this point in the argument, the interpreter insists that the bridge was always there, leaning *forward* from Old Testament promise to New Testament fulfillment. This is usually asserted despite the fact that the newly revealed connections never appeared in any pre-Christian interpretive traditions, which by itself ought to make readers suspect that such interpretive projects are begging the question. Is it not suspicious that only Christians have ever discovered these New Testament–like elements of messianic prediction in the Old Testament?

D. A. Carson's efforts to make sense of Matthew 2:15 are typical.[37] He begins by arguing that Matthew's idea of "fulfillment" must be understood in light of the "interlocking themes and their typological connections" identifying Jesus as the Messiah. His exposition of these themes and typological connections, however, draws exclusively on Matthew, Hebrews, and Paul's letters. Though Old Testament texts are cited parenthetically, exposition of them depends entirely on New Testament theology. Any apparent disjunction between expectation and fulfillment is eliminated as the two different horizons (Old and New Testaments) are forcibly fused and flattened into one.

---

35. See the examples discussed below.

36. Typology in biblical interpretation involves the understanding of some characters and stories in the Old Testament as allegories foreshadowing events in the New Testament.

37. *Matthew* (Expositor's Bible Commentary 8; Grand Rapids: Zondervan, 1984) 91-93.

Carson concludes that because Hosea was situated within a broad "messianic matrix" scattered throughout the Old Testament, we can confidently assume that the "messianic nuances" of his reference to "my son" were self-evident to the prophet,[38] never mind that Hosea had his own context as a pre-exilic prophet![39] Thus, even though Carson confesses that Matthew's "fuller meaning" only becomes apparent "in retrospect," the Gospel writer's interpretation of Hosea is nonetheless legitimate since he is elucidating "the pattern of revelation up to that time — a pattern not yet adequately discerned."[40]

The "pattern" linking the Old and the New is finally revealed. But, despite claims that this messianic pattern originates from the Old Testament side of the divide, the logic by which it has been woven moves backward from the New Testament to the Old. Even the claim that Hosea's reference to "my son" (cf. Exod. 4:22-23; Ps. 2:7) is necessarily messianic depends on knowledge of such New Testament passages as Romans 1:1-4 and Hebrews 1:1-9[41] and is not supportable by Old Testament evidence alone.[42]

---

38. Actually, he fudges on this point: "Hosea, building on existing revelation, grasped the messianic nuances of the 'son' language already applied to Israel and David's promised heir in previous revelation so that had he been able to see Matthew's use of 11:1, he would not have disapproved, even if messianic nuances were not in his mind when he wrote that verse" (92). But if the prophet grasped the messianic nuances of "my son," why wouldn't they be in his mind when he wrote 11:1? And how do we know what was in the author's mind apart from what he wrote?

39. That is, Hosea's ministry is previous to the exile of the Jews to Babylon in about 600 B.C. and as such his words are best understood in that historical context rather than the one Matthew borrows them for.

40. *Matthew,* 93.

41. ". . . the gospel he promised beforehand through his prophets in the Holy Scriptures regarding his Son . . . who through the Spirit of holiness was declared with power to be the Son of God" (Rom. 1:2-3); "In the past God spoke to our forefathers through the prophets . . . but in these last days he has spoken to us by his Son. . . . The Son is the radiance of God's glory . . ." (Heb. 1:1-3).

42. For a related discussion of Matthew's use of Hos. 11:1, see J. H. Sailhamer, "Hosea 11:1 and Matthew 2:15," *Westminster Theological Journal* 63 (2001): 87-96, followed on pp. 97-105 by a thorough critique by D. McCartney and P. Enns. McCartney and Enns similarly observe that "our ability to see [a] trajectory from our Christian vantage point cannot be used to argue that the trajectory can be found in the Pentateuch via grammatical-historical exegesis without reference to the NT" (97-98).

What Is Going On Here?

Historians are uncomfortable with intractable instances of historical discontinuity. This is the root of the problem at hand. Historical method always looks for some account of cause and effect to explain how action A propelled the occasion for reaction B.[43] Biblical studies as a discipline operates with similar expectations. The historical methodology inclines biblical scholars to search for some historical "middle term" that can stand between the pre-Christian expectations that never anticipated anyone like Jesus Christ and the apostolic preaching insisting that Jesus alone fulfills Old Testament expectations. The historical Jesus himself proves to be the "middle term"[44] between these two sides of the historical chasm. Even so, no matter how subtly one reconstructs the man from Nazareth, no matter how convincing the arguments for his genius in rereading the Old Testament and applying it to himself, no factual, historical "middle term" can adequately explain why any first-century Jew would have (a) confessed this crucified man as Messiah and (b) accepted the messianic interpretations in the New Testament as legitimate accounts of Old Testament fulfillment. Inserting the historical Jesus between one side of the chasm and the other only defers a real solution and simply does not answer the looming questions. In fact, no historical claim, on its own, is sufficient to answer these questions. For the problem of fulfillment not only concerns the historical plausibility of the (reconstructed) historical Jesus but must also answer adequately the religious and existential dimensions — the faith dimensions — the figure of Jesus is being asked to bear. It's a question not only of scientific accuracy but of how all historical "middle

43. This is equally true for both the skeptical application of historical criticism as well as the conservative use of grammatical-historical exegesis, both of which share a common ancestry in Enlightenment rationalism.

44. I borrow the phrase "middle term" from Wright, *Jesus*, 592, who says, "In order to move, as historians, from the Jewish world to the very similar, and yet very different, world of early Christianity, we have to postulate a middle term." The middle term he then offers is a portrayal of the historical Jesus built by way of his own analysis of the Gospels. Although I am grateful for Wright's judicious reading of the Evangelists and his prudent judgments on historical questions, I must take issue (if I understand his argument correctly) with the common enough notion that one's view of the historical Jesus (however critically or conservatively constructed) can function as a sufficient middle term to bridge the historical gap separating the "Jewish world" from the "world of early Christianity." Traversing between those two sides is not a mere "matter of scientific, historical judgment" (593).

terms" and all the unprecedented claims of the earliest disciples hold up under scrutiny.

No historical information per se will ever reduce this historical gap. Historical investigation is crucial, but it can only take us so far. Crossing over from the Old Testament / pre-Jesus position to a New Testament / post-Jesus situation demands an individual leap of faith. Is the individual willing to keep in step with God's activity even when it is completely unforeseen?

We have come full circle. We must swallow the pill and choose to exchange illusion for historical *terra firma*. In that case we will accept that *the historical evidence is such that historical evidence alone cannot explain the earliest disciples' faith in Jesus as Messiah*. Human understanding must confess the limits of its understanding.

Leaping between the Testaments

What do Kierkegaard and first-century Jewish messianic expectations have to do with each other?[45] Both can teach us something about jumping. Kierkegaard is commonly associated with the idea of faith as a leap, a blind leap into the anti-intellectual arms of irrational religion. Leaping suggests the last-ditch efforts of someone who has abandoned all hope of finding reasonable answers to life's questions. One will jump from the roof of a burning building only when there is no other option, only as a final act of desperation. However, despite its popularity, this picture of Kierkegaard is a serious misunderstanding of how he describes the nature of faith. He is rightly famous for emphasizing the importance of subjectivity and per-

45. Readers familiar with Kierkegaard may notice that I am making a significant modification to his arguments about faith. He most consistently links faith's paradoxical nature (or its "absurdity") to the incarnation, frequently claiming that it was Jesus' own claims to divinity that created the chief barrier to his acceptance among his Jewish contemporaries. Thus faith in Jesus is always a leap because reason alone can never explain how this particular individual is the God-man. However, by reading the four Gospels primarily through the doctrinal lens of Christ's two natures, Kierkegaard allows his Christological orthodoxy to overwhelm a careful historical reading of the Gospels themselves. Jesus' claims to messiahship, such as they were, did not present him as God in the flesh but as the Deliverer no one expected. The incarnation would certainly become a decisive faith issue for later generations of believers, but not for the immediate contemporaries of the earthly Jesus. Their questions concerned the lack of correlation between Jesus' career and Jewish expectations.

sonal decision in taking the step of faith. But faith is not an act of panic, not the enemy of reason, and not anti-intellectual.[46]

According to Kierkegaard, "faith is immediacy after reflection."[47] *Immediacy* in this context is his word for personal appropriation or ownership, what he elsewhere likes to call passion. *Reflection* is shorthand for the individual's thoughtful consideration of the different arguments pointing our decision-making processes in one direction or another. The key to this definition of faith is the relationship between the two poles of faith and reason. Immediacy and reflection are equally important. Neither can produce faith on its own. The order in which they appear is also crucial. Faith is always immediacy *after* reflection. Immediacy without reflection is not faith but enthusiasm subject to the dangers of passionate ignorance. Mass hysteria is an example. On the other hand, imagining that immediacy can be created by reflection produces neither faith nor true immediacy but a dead orthodoxy. Suggesting that reflection alone may lead to faith makes as much sense as believing that memorizing the Declaration of Independence will turn the student into a Founding Father. Analyzing evidence, calculating historical probabilities, considering philosophical alternatives, and every other application of our God-given reason are all important, but none of them in and of itself will ever carry an individual across the divide that separates information from personal commitment. Only the willful risk of choosing faith can do that. *Immediacy* prevents faith from being confused with an intellectual consent that leaves lifestyle or decision-making completely unaffected. *Reflection* ensures that faith is knowingly and responsibly chosen as one's own and is not just an artifact of cultural conditioning or an accident of birth.

Now we are in a better position to understand Kierkegaard's usefulness to the present discussion, for the chasm waiting to be crossed by the

---

46. For an excellent discussion of the relationship between faith and reason in Kierkegaard's thinking, see C. S. Evans, *Passionate Reason: Making Sense of Kierkegaard's Philosophical Fragments* (Bloomington: Indiana University Press, 1992), and *Faith beyond Reason: A Kierkegaardian Account* (Grand Rapids: Eerdmans, 1998).

47. *The Journals of Kierkegaard, 1834-1854* (ed. and trans. A. Dru; London: Fontana, 1960) 140, 142; for a discussion of what Kierkegaard intends by referring to faith as a "second immediacy," see J. H. Thomas, *Subjectivity and Paradox: A Study of Kierkegaard* (Oxford: Blackwell, 1957) 98-102. For a broader description of the roles played by both immediacy and reflection throughout Kierkegaard's authorship, see M. Taylor, "Sounds of Silence," in *Kierkegaard's* Fear and Trembling: *Critical Appraisals* (ed. R. Perkins; Tuscaloosa: University of Alabama Press, 1981) 165-88.

earliest disciples demanded a leap of faith. For Peter, James, and John, as well as Kierkegaard, the challenge of faith is a challenge inherent to the nature of history.

Kierkegaard raises two historical questions, although he does not always distinguish between them, and the first is often hidden in the second. First, how reliable must historical information be before it can reasonably serve as the basis for religious belief? Second, can any historical event, no matter how certain, legitimately function as the basis for faith?[48] Kierkegaard answers these questions by explaining why Christian faith must be a leap. Calculating the reasonableness of faith against historical reliability is a fool's errand because no historical event, no matter how certain the empirical evidence, can compel anyone to stake their eternal destiny on it.

> Even if it were the most certain of all historical facts it would be of no help, there cannot be any *direct* transition from an historical fact to the foundation upon it of an eternal happiness. That is something qualitatively new. . . .
>
> And so I say to myself: I choose; that historical fact means so much to me that I decide to stake my whole life upon that if. Then he lives; lives entirely full of the idea, risking his life for it; and his life is the proof that he believes. He did not have a few proofs, and so believed and then began to live. No, the very reverse.
>
> That is called risking; and without risk faith is an impossibility.[49]

48. Kierkegaard is responding directly to the famous declaration of G. Lessing: "Accidental truths of history can never become the proof of necessary truths of reason." See "On the Proof of the Spirit and of Power," in *Lessing's Theological Writings* (ed. and trans. H. Chadwick; Stanford: Stanford University Press, 1967) 53. For Kierkegaard's analysis and response, see his *Philosophical Fragments* and *Concluding Unscientific Postscript to Philosophical Fragments*. Kierkegaard never questions the historical reliability of the canonical Gospels. Consequently, questions of historical criticism are overlooked in his presentation of the necessarily subjective nature of faith. Although this might be taken to imply that historical veracity and the objective dimension of religious truth claims are irrelevant to Christian faith, Kierkegaard insists on the objective reality of Christian truth; for only one example see *The Book on Adler* (Princeton: Princeton University Press, 1998) 117-18: "The essentially Christian exists before any Christian exists; it must exist in order for one to become a Christian. It contains the qualification by which a test is made of whether someone has become a Christian; it maintains its objective continuance outside all believers, while also it is in the inwardness of the believer. In short, here there is no identity between the subjective and the objective."

49. *The Journals*, 184-85.

Kierkegaard envisions a qualitative gap: on the one side are the merely probable details of historical evidence; on the other side are the absolute professions of religious conviction. No amount of historical investigation can ever guarantee the validity of religious belief, since history deals only with varying levels of probability, and probability never strong-arms anyone to an inescapable, necessary conclusion. To think otherwise is a bit like alchemy, imagining that molten lead can be transformed into gold *if only* it is stirred vigorously enough. Historical probabilities alone can never provide unquestionable certainty about the object of faith. At some point, the believer simply must act, choose. Historical evidence is not irrelevant to this decision and may have crucial significance for the way reflection urges us to immediacy. But in the end the decision itself is never inescapable, either logically or historically. It is always deliberate, contingent, and uncertain. The transition from historical probability to personal profession demands that each individual take the risk of jumping — not proving, not reasoning — from one side of the chasm to the other and then living with the consequences of that decision.

Kierkegaard was addressing the need for a radical redefinition of faith among nineteenth-century theologians (especially the followers of Hegel), biblical critics, and adherents to the Danish state church. He was convinced that baptismal records and seminary diplomas registered with the local parish were not evidence of faith. His call was to abandon the arrogant quest for historical certainty and intellectual mastery in exchange for risking eternity on childlike trust in Christ.

Jesus' Jewish contemporaries also needed to embrace a major revolution in their messianic expectations.[50] Jesus would never satisfy anyone's religious expectations for a coming Messiah. Consequently, the leap required of them was of the same sort as that demanded of Kierkegaard's neighbors in Copenhagen, though the nature of the expectation gap was quite different. The chasm between Old Testament religious expectation and New Testament realization was the result not of historical uncertainty but of historical disparity. But in both cases the leap of faith requires the same immediacy after reflection. For the first-century Jewish audience, re-

50. The term "paradigm shift" was first used by Thomas Kuhn his influential book *The Structure of Scientific Revolutions* (Chicago: University of Chicago Press, 1962). It typically describes a revolutionary transformation in the way one thinks about a problem, such as the shift from a geocentric to a heliocentric view of the universe or the change from a Newtonian to an Einsteinian understanding of gravity, space, and time.

flection on the nature of Jesus involved both the risk of being wrong about the Messiah and *the abandonment of all prior religious expectations for the idiosyncratic claims of a wandering carpenter named Jesus.*[51]

Jumping Backward

This first-century leap of faith was a leap toward the idiosyncratic way in which the New Testament writers recast the entire Old Testament. Once they had crossed the chasm of their failed expectations, the earliest disciples found themselves in new existential territory offering a new vantage point from which to reread and reinterpret both their heritage and their place in it. Reconsidering their prior understanding of their sacred texts required a long, hard look back at their traditions. Holding on to the authority of the Hebrew Scriptures while leaping to embrace Jesus as Messiah demanded that these two previously disparate faith statements be reconciled. If Jesus was the Messiah, then the details of his life and ministry, no matter how surprising, must be discernible somehow in the pages of Scripture — shouldn't they? Thus the initial existential leap became the premise for a second leap, an essential interpretive leap. The first leap places faith in Jesus as the surprising fulfillment of God's promises. The second turns back again and rearticulates faith in God's promises as they actually have been fulfilled in Jesus. The first leap reveals how faith expresses immediacy after reflection. The second reveals how New Testament faith reinterprets Old Testament texts in new ways. This biblical intertextuality expresses *the gospel imagination after faith.*

The disciples walking the Emmaus Road (Luke 24:13-35) illustrate both stages of this process.[52] First, the reader is reminded that Jesus' crucifixion and entombment bore no relation to the disciples' traditional expectations. Their traditional hopes were once stirred by Jesus, but now they were thoroughly disheartened by recent events, and the dissonance between expectation and reality rings out in their lament, "We hoped that he was going to be the One to redeem Israel" (v. 21). The stage was set for

51. Chapter 3 will explore the various dynamics involved in making this exchange while spanning the qualitative gap by faith.

52. I provide a more detailed analysis of the Emmaus narrative in *Jesus the Intercessor: Prayer and Christology in Luke-Acts* (Tübingen: Mohr, 1992; Grand Rapids: Baker, 1999) 98-108.

the initial, existential leap of faith. In this instance, that new understanding is deferred by divine intervention (v. 16: "their eyes had been closed so that they could not recognize him"), so it is not the encounter alone but the accompanying biblical exposition that eventually opens their eyes. Their encounter with the resurrected Jesus must transform everything they once thought they knew about Israel's Redeemer. Jesus himself rereads the Scriptures in light of his cross and empty tomb (vv. 25-27, 32); he personally demonstrates the second, interpretive leap of faith, reaffirming the authority of Scripture in light of its fulfillment. Emmaus is a paradigm for the method of biblical interpretation through reinterpretation (intertextuality). Emmaus lays down what becomes the normal sequence, the move from existential experience to reinterpretation in a leap of faith.[53]

Even though scholars have long recognized that the New Testament writers interpret the Old Testament in light of Christ and the gospel message,[54] a serious inconsistency regularly appears in the literature. While paying lip service to the idea of reading the Old Testament in light of Christ, some scholars are as uncomfortable with this second interpretive leap of faith. Two points are frequently made simultaneously: (a) the New Testament's use of the Old Testament is only understandable in the light of Christ, and (b) the Old Testament, in and of itself, points to the work of Jesus. But these claims are contradictory. Either the Old Testament is

---

53. C. H. Dodd, *According to the Scriptures: The Substructure of New Testament Theology* (Digswell Place: Nisbet, 1952) 110, describing the creativity of the New Testament use of the Old Testament, observes, "This is a piece of genuinely creative thinking. Who was responsible for it? The early Church, we are accustomed to say, and perhaps we can safely say no more. But creative thinking is rarely done by committees. . . . The New Testament itself avers that it was Jesus Christ Himself who first directed the minds of His followers to certain parts of the scriptures. . . . I can see no reasonable ground for rejecting the statements of the gospels. . . . To account for the beginning of this most original and fruitful process of rethinking the Old Testament we found need to postulate a creative mind. The Gospels offer us one. Are we compelled to reject the offer?" In my opinion, nothing has been learned or discovered in the six decades to challenge Dodd's conclusions. See also R. T. France, *Jesus and the Old Testament: His Application of the Old Testament Passages to Himself and His Mission* (London: Tyndale, 1971).

54. K. Snodgrass, "The Use of the Old Testament in the New," in *New Testament Criticism and Interpretation* (ed. D. Black and D. Dockery; Grand Rapids: Zondervan, 1991) 418, puts it well when he says, "The conviction about [Jesus'] identity did *not* derive from the Old Testament. [The New Testament authors] did not find texts and then find Jesus. They found Jesus and then saw how the Scriptures fit with him. They were not *proving* his identity in the technical sense so much as they were demonstrating how the Scriptures fit with him."

properly understood only in light of Jesus' actual manner of fulfillment, or it points to the ministry of Jesus in a comprehensible manner by predicting what he would do. We cannot have it both ways. We may accept one or the other claim or neither, but not both (a) that Jesus fulfilled the Old Testament in ways that were not anticipated and (b) that the Old Testament predicted what Jesus actually did. An example will help to clarify this contradiction.

In his programmatic essay "The Problem of *Sensus Plenior,*" Douglas Moo admits that typological[55] readings of the Old Testament, that is, readings that see a deeper fulfillment in Jesus of an Old Testament narrative, often "appear to be arbitrary applications of Old Testament texts." He cites the New Testament use of Psalm 22 in Mark 15:34; Matthew 27:46; and John 19:24 as an example, explaining that David's "individual lament" typologically anticipates the suffering of Jesus. Though "it is not clear that David would always have been aware of the ultimate significance of his language," we can trust that "God had so ordered his experiences and his recording of them in Scripture" such that they intentionally prefigured the suffering of Jesus.[56]

Reading such typology into the New Testament may initially create the impression of theological disjunction between the two testaments. However, Moo assures his readers that such hints of disparity are more apparent than real. The explanation, he says, is that "typology does have a 'pro-

55. The classic discussion of typology is still L. Goppelt, *Typos: The Typological Interpretation of the Old Testament in the New* (trans. D. H. Madvig; Grand Rapids: Eerdmans, 1982), originally published in 1939. Goppelt's definition of typology contains three essential elements. First, narrative details such as persons, actions, events, and institutions are seen to correspond to each other, one (type or prototype) in the Old Testament, the other (antitype) in the New Testament. Second, not only does the type look forward to the antitype, but the significance of the antitype is escalated or augmented beyond the significance of the type. Third, the antitype appears in connection with the time of eschatological fulfillment (17-20). A crucial note in Goppelt's study, frequently overlooked, is his insistence that typology does not offer a method but a way of seeing: "typology is not a hermeneutical method to be used in a technical way to interpret the OT. It is a spiritual approach that reveals the connection ordained in God's redemptive plan. . . . The result is not a typological system but is clearly an insight" (223).

56. D. Moo, "The Problem of *Sensus Plenior,*" in *Hermeneutics, Authority, and Canon* (ed. D. A. Carson and J. D. Woodbridge; Grand Rapids: Baker, 1995) 198. The implicit assumptions underlying this sentence are remarkable. In fact, Psalm 22 gives us no reason to assume that David (if he in fact wrote Psalm 22) was in any way ever aware of what "the ultimate significance of his language" would become for the New Testament!

spective' element, but the 'prospective' nature of specific Old Testament incidents could often be recognized only retrospectively."[57] If you follow Moo, any theological conflicts seemingly created by the retrospective interpretations that arise from the New Testament's use of the Old are only apparent. Potential typological elements in the Old Testament are found to have deeper meanings which the New Testament writers were the first to recognize retrospectively. In other words, what had previously remained unrecognized is now seen accurately in retrospect! Furthermore, these potential meanings of the Old Testament went unrecognized because they were *intended* to be recognized only retrospectively. This, too, was a part of God's plan.

Such explanations of typology and retrospective fulfillment strike me as highly problematic. How can something be prospective if it was intentionally recognizable only in retrospect? "Prospective" normally indicates that a clue is embedded to help the reader anticipate what is coming next. But if such an indicator is recognizable only after the fact, it has failed to indicate and its potential for suggestion is empty. It is like a highway exit sign that becomes visible only after the exit. Yet this is how some scholars would have us understand the New Testament interpretation of "prospective" elements in the Old Testament.

It is not uncommon to read scholars using creative descriptions of the various ways in which the Old Testament anticipates, points to, models, or prefigures the New Testament or is latent or pregnant with specific meanings that only become visible in the light of Christ's fulfillment. But it is an odd preparation that fails to prepare or an odd prediction that does not predict in any recognizable fashion.[58] When nothing within the Old Testa-

---

57. "The Problem," 197. The article is littered with similar methodological oxymorons.

58. Another error is also at work here, a type of category confusion. This logical mistake operates whenever general Old Testament expectations are too easily linked with specific elements of the gospel. For example, describing the general category of a Messiah like Moses who leads a second exodus, or a Messiah like David seated on God's throne, occurs at a different level of specificity than that required of someone who chooses to embrace the crucified, resurrected, and exalted Jesus as the final, royal prophet. Unfolding a general typology within the Old Testament is a far cry from demonstrating that it anticipated or pointed to its specific antitypical fulfillment in Jesus. This may seem obvious, but it bears repeating. Yes, the Gospels depict Calvary as the exodus of the final Moses and the seat of Christ's enthronement, but the Evangelists' understanding of the cross has nothing to do with recognizing patterns in history, knowing how to read typology, or comparing type to antitype. It has only to do with faith and the perceptions enabled by that faith.

ment text *as text* seemingly refers to the crucified and exalted Jesus Christ apart from a previous experience with Christ through faith, then we have no choice but to look for a way to *leap* from the New Testament to the Old Testament, just as the first generation of disciples was compelled to leap from the Old Testament to Jesus as Messiah. First came faith, and then came a newly created gospel imagination activated by that faith.

Look before You Leap

Richard Hays's *Echoes of Scripture in the Letters of Paul* offers an especially insightful study of Paul's approach to Old Testament interpretation. Though Hays has a few moments where he, too, lapses into the type of contradiction described above,[59] his study is noteworthy for its thoughtful consistency and lucid, creative exposition. Though he travels by a different route, Hays also embraces the imagery of leaping to describe Paul's method of scriptural interpretation:

> There is no evidence in the letters that Paul — in contrast to other ancient authors such as Philo — ever sat down with the biblical text and tried to figure out what it might mean by applying an exegetical procedure abstractable from the particular text that he was reading. Rather, he seems to have *leaped* — in moments of metaphorical insight — to *intuitive* apprehensions to the meanings of texts.[60]

A leap directed by intuition describes not only what Paul was doing but the practice of every other New Testament writer as well. Time and again, the correspondence between old and new, whether labeled type and antitype (typology), vehicle and tenor (metaphor), or promise and fulfillment (prophecy), is not proven or demonstrated by the New Testament

---

59. Having already asserted that "scripture can be understood appropriately only in Christ" (*Echoes*, 148), that it is only understandable "under the guidance of the Spirit as a witness to the gospel" (149), Hays goes on to describe how the Old Testament "signifies far more than it says," disclosing "[i]ts latent sense . . . only to those to those who 'turn to the Lord'" (154). Again, I suggest that a latent signification that is only recognizable as such after the fact is neither truly latent nor a genuine signifier. The oxymoron's grip shows itself again, even in Hays's otherwise perspicuous study.

60. *Echoes*, 160-61, emphasis added; see similar analysis on 88, 94, 100-121.

author as much as it is asserted through a hermeneutical act of the will.[61] In this way, both the existential embrace of the gospel and the interpretive commitment to reading Scripture through the eyes of that same gospel are equally willful and subjective. Both are passionate acts of faith. The latter is a willful decision to read the Old Testament in a way commensurate with the willful decision to have faith in Christ. Thus the New Testament writer insists "This is that. Period. Believe it." Christ *is* the Suffering Servant (1 Pet. 2:21-25). The church *is* the true Israel (Gal. 6:16; Rom. 9:22–10:21). Paul's Gentile mission *is* an element of Christ restoring David's throne (Acts 15:15-18). Of course, all these intuitive apprehensions leave the reader asking an obvious question. How does the author know this? By what draftsman's tool has the author drawn this particular straight line from this New Testament point A to that Old Testament point B? What force has directed the trajectory of this interpretive leap?

Exercising a Gospel Imagination

Scholars have come to the realization that biblical interpretation within Second Temple Judaism is incredibly complex and sophisticated. This research has identified specific characteristics of Jewish exegetical methods. When we trace methodological parallels between the New Testament writers and other ancient Jewish writers, several distinct approaches to interpretation are revealed. In the New Testament readers can discern

> *midrash,* a homiletic approach that interprets biblical stories by filling in many gaps left in the biblical narrative,
> *pesher,* which interprets Scripture on two levels, a surface level and a concealed level that is usually of immediate relevance and that is for those with higher knowledge,
> *haggadah,* exposition by way of an explanatory story, and
> allegory, communication with symbolic figures, actions, or representations.[62]

---

61. I agree completely with Hays, *Echoes,* 82 when he says, "Paul's interpretation presupposes what it argues and argues what it presupposes. . . . The argument, at its explicit level, rests on sheer force of assertion."

62. J. W. Doeve, *Jewish Hermeneutics in the Synoptic Gospels and Acts* (Assen: Van

However, cataloguing methodological similarities does not answer the more basic question of "Why?" Why *this* pattern? Why *that* correspondence? Describing the different tools available to an ancient craftsman cannot account for the creative inspiration behind any particular work of art. Each brush or chisel, no matter how common, was held in the hand of a uniquely gifted artist. Why did *this* artist put *that* brushstroke precisely *there?* Why was *that* chisel chosen to carve *this* groove *here* in *that* particular way? The answer is undoubtedly as idiosyncratic as the artist. Years of apprenticeship spent learning proper technique are combined with personal inspiration.

Hays argues that the creative inspiration directing Paul's interpretive leaps — his exegetical brushstrokes, if you will — arose from his ecclesiology, that is, his belief that the church is the new community of God's people. Paul "makes the biblical text pass through the filter of his experience of God's action of forming the church."[63] Looking for points of continuity between his experience in the local church and the Old Testament's depiction of God's covenant people Israel, Paul leaps the interpretive chasm. He draws his creative lines of theological connection accordingly. The problem with Hays's solution, as I see it, is that it merely describes the interpretive effects. Hays does not penetrate far enough to uncover the first cause of those effects. This approach can be compared to the butcher who says that he creates T-bone steaks while never thinking to remind his customers that a living, breathing steer stood at the beginning of the steak-making process.

Similarly, it is the experience of Christ himself that produces the church. Without an experience of the gospel of Jesus Christ shared among its members, there is no such thing as the church. Although Hays recognizes this fact, he stops short of allowing the primacy of this individual faith decision to have its rightful place as the key to biblical interpretation.

Gorcum, 1954); E. E. Ellis, *Paul's Use of the Old Testament* (London: Oliver and Boyd, 1957) 38-76, 139-49; *Prophecy and Hermeneutic in Early Christianity* (Tübingen: Mohr, 1978) 147-81, 188-208; *The Old Testament in Early Christianity: Canon and Interpretation in the Light of Modern Research* (Tübingen: Mohr, 1991) 77-103, 130-38; G. Vermes, *Scripture and Tradition in Judaism: Haggadic Studies* (Leiden: Brill, 1973) 193-27; *Jesus in His Jewish Context* (Minneapolis: Fortress, 2003) 114-23; *Scrolls, Scriptures and Early Christianity* (London: Clark, 2005) 44-79; D. Instone-Brewer, *Techniques and Assumptions in Jewish Exegesis before 70 CE* (Tübingen: Mohr, 1992).

63. *Echoes*, 102; see the sections on ecclesiocentric hermeneutics in 84-87, 105-21.

He doesn't allow this decision to be the first cause behind all consequent interpretative choices. To say that Scripture is only understood properly in light of its fulfillment in Christ implies the personal, existential leap that brings each individual into life with Christ and into the larger fellowship of the Christian church. This very relation is at the root of the creative, inspirational genius igniting the intuitive leap from the New Testament's reading of the Old Testament. The New Testament writers read the Old Testament through the lens of a gospel-inspired imagination activated by the Holy Spirit. They do not exhibit a particular method of reading as much as they do a distinctive way of seeing. The existential leap is the mother of the interpretive leap.

Mastering technique did not teach Michelangelo how to sculpt his Florentine David. His tools and technique, as masterful as they were, required the inspiration of a unique, artistic imagination, an ability to recognize the figure long entombed within the white, Carrara marble awaiting liberation through his genius at interpreting the stone. The gospel imagination served a similar purpose for the New Testament readers of the Old Testament.

Let me try a more mundane illustration.

When I was a young boy, breakfast often included the discovery of an inexpensive new toy, something dug out of the recently purchased cereal box. Along with an overdose of sugar, to seduce young consumers the cereal companies included small gadgets in every box to lure hapless mothers back to the same aisle of the grocery store as their children would beg them to buy another box of cereal next week.

I remember the first time I found a secret decoder kit in my cereal. It was a small square of red-tinted plastic that revealed the hidden message waiting to be unveiled on a small square of white cardboard. The cardboard did not appear to hold any information, but when a child placed the red plastic on top of it, a secret message was suddenly revealed. However, if you looked hard enough you might be able to make out barely visible orange lines inscribed on the cardboard; it was not truly blank. But the top-secret message only became clearly visible after being revealed by the translucent red overlay placed on top of the white square.

That is how I used to think of the New Testament's relation to the Old Testament. I believed that a "preview" of Jesus Christ was available within the pages of the Old Testament. However, it required the "overlay" of New Testament fulfillment before the Messiah's disguised outline and subtle shading were sufficiently enhanced to become clearly visible. Only then could one discern how Jesus of Nazareth actually comports with Old Testament expectations. According to this understanding, it was appropriate to describe New Testament acts of fulfillment as prefigured in the Old Testament.

I am now convinced that my analogy needs adjustment, or even to be turned on its head. I still understand the Old Testament to be that white cardboard and the red-tinted plastic square still can be seen as Jesus and the New Testament, but I now understand that the new interpretation is not hidden on the cardboard. It is drawn onto the piece of plastic. There is no decoding process where something secret is finally revealed; no invisible ink is magically made visible. The Messiah's image and the significance of his work are inscribed only on the New Testament overlay. The Christian Messiah becomes discernible only when placed on top of the Old Testament "cardboard" with its variety of symbols, imagery, and competing expectations. However, the specifics of Christ's accomplishments do not arise from the Old Testament, not even proleptically. Rather, they exist independently of that background and are imposed on it by gospel history. The claims of messianic fulfillment are highlighted most starkly when juxtaposed against the Old Testament literature, but their existence and visibility are not dependent on those writings. The messianic fulfillment of Jesus Christ is the gospel-tinted overlay placed on the Old Testament by the creativity of the New Testament writers who viewed life and their own sacred texts through a gospel-inspired imagination.

The New Testament's approach to interpreting the Old Testament is similar to the *pesher* method applied at Qumran.[64] Those who wrote these

64. The similarities between the New Testament writers' approach to Old Testament interpretation and the methods adopted by the Qumran community are well known; some, but not all, of these similarities may also be found with rabbinic methods. (1) Both the church and Qumran gathered around a charismatic leader/founder who handed down a creative, "inspired" method of interpreting Scripture; as F. F. Bruce, *Biblical Exegesis in the Qumran Texts* (Grand Rapids: Eerdmans, 1959) 67 says, if the apostles had been asked where they learned their interpretive method, "they would have acknowledged that they had received it from Jesus. In this respect Jesus was to the early church what the Teacher of Righteousness was to the Qumran community." (2) Biblical interpretation in both communities could be called "charismatic" in the sense that interpretation itself was a revelatory event born of the interpreter's faith commitment. (3) The final authority of any Old Testament text did not reside in the text alone but in its correct interpretation, which was now available exclusively within the new community (compare 1 Cor. 3:4-18). (4) Both groups believed

pesharim or interpretations believed that Scripture was written on two levels, the surface level for ordinary readers and the concealed level, reserved for specialists with higher or special knowledge, which explained how the text was currently being fulfilled in the group offering the interpretation. So the early church was only one group of sectarian Jews who saw themselves as the principal subject of Old Testament prophecy. The Qumran Covenanters (those making up the community that wrote many of the Dead Sea Scrolls), like the early Christians, shared a similar faith: "We are the fulfillment" might well be their assertion. They would assert that the developments "among us" are the realization of the word in the prophets. "Our experience with our spiritual leader," whether that leader be the Teacher of Righteousness of the Dead Sea Scrolls or Jesus of Nazareth, "is the end-time realization of all the prophetic hopes and dreams." It seems likely that the currency of these shared attitudes among the Essenes (another term for the people of the Dead Sea Scrolls) at Qumran and Jesus' disciples helps to explain the New Testament assertion that the Father sent his Son "in the fullness of time" (Rom. 5:6; 2 Cor. 6:2; Gal. 4:4; Eph. 1:10; 1 Tim. 2:6; Heb. 1:1-2).

Such an expectation of the fullness of time is clearly also at work with the Jews of Qumran.[65] This contemporary recontextualization of the Old Testament is apparent, for example, in a text such as 1QpHab 7:1-5, which comments on Habakkuk 2:2, "God told Habakkuk to write down the

---

that they were God's eschatological community living in the final age of fulfillment. (5) The true intention of Scripture is always to address the interpreter's immediate, contemporary situation (see Rom. 4:23-24; 15:4; 1 Cor. 9:10; 10:6, 11; Jude 1:4). (6) Since the church and Qumran were both living in the age of fulfillment, the Old Testament promises were being fulfilled among them within their own historical experience. For further elaboration of these points, see Bruce, *Biblical Exegesis*, 7-17, 66-77; K. Stendahl, *The School of St. Matthew and Its Use of the Old Testament* (Philadelphia: Fortress, 1968) 183-202; Ellis, *Paul's Use*, 140-49; *Prophecy*, 147-81, 188-97; *The Old Testament*, 77-121; Juel, *Messianic Exegesis*, 31-57; D. N. Freedman, "Prophecy in the Dead Sea Scrolls," in Charlesworth and Weaver, ed., *Dead Sea Scrolls and Christian Faith*, 42-57; J. H. Charlesworth, *The Pesharim and Qumran History: Chaos or Consensus?* (Grand Rapids: Eerdmans, 2002) 2-16, 67-77; T. Lim, *Pesharim* (London: Sheffield Academic, 2002) 24-26; Vermes, *Scrolls*, 44-79.

65. In the Dead Sea Scrolls the Hebrew word *pesher* ("interpretation") is used for works of biblical commentary; in the course of explanation it becomes a linking word that introduces "an interpretation [of a biblical passage] in which the text is applied to the author's own historical context, which is believed to be situated in the 'end of days'"; see D. Dimant, "Pesharim," in Collins and Harlow, eds., *Eerdmans Dictionary of Early Judaism*, 1050.

things that are going to come upon the last generation. . . . Its interpretation *(pesher)* concerns the Teacher of Righteousness [the Qumran community's founder], that God made known to him all the mysteries of the words of his servants the prophets." Obviously, the hermeneutical pathway followed by the early Christians was already well-traveled. The church's existential reading of the Old Testament had echoes in the passionate readings of other Jewish groups at the time. It really is not too hard to image the church's existential leap of faith if you compare it to the interpretive world of early Judaism.

Living Forward, Understanding Backward

> life can only be understood backward
> it must be lived forward

Those words on the screen in a trailer for *The Curious Case of Benjamin Button* convinced me to see the film. I do not know if the advertisers deliberately quoted Kierkegaard, but I was curious to discover if Mr. Button's "curious case" would explain what the curious Dane had meant by those words.

The movie left me disappointed. Benjamin Button is born old, ages in reverse, and dies a helpless newborn tended by his aged and devoted wife. The young and elderly Benjamin brings no wisdom or experience with him into the world, although his life does teach him that he is headed to an eventual infant death. He lives his life backward, which is indeed curious. But the old and youthful Benjamin becomes a callow, rebellious boy who not only lacks wisdom (still) but eventually forgets everything he ever knew. He lives forward-backward and never truly benefits from life's experience, either backward or forward. This is certainly curious, but not what Kierkegaard had in mind.

Kierkegaard insists that, ultimately, life is only grasped from the vantage point of eternity. Only God understands the true meaning of each individual's existence, and only a relationship with God provides the viewpoint from which to see the truth of one's life.[66]

---

66. *The Journals,* 89. I am drawing on Kierkegaard's concept of repetition but not reproducing it exactly. I believe it makes for a useful analogy. Kierkegaard developed the idea

Life must be understood backwards. But [philosophers] forget the other proposition, that it must be lived forwards. And if one thinks over that proposition it becomes more and more evident that life can never really be understood in time simply because at no particular moment can I find the necessary resting-place from which to understand it — backwards.

In other words, life must forever remain mysterious and uncertain, at least in this world. It is never fully comprehended within time, partly because it remains unfinished, partly because time never provides a solid, unchangeable platform from which to stand and take stock. Every moment slips away into the next and is altered by what intervenes. Successive choices and decisions propel us into the unknown, while moments of deepening reflection on what we have done and who we have become blossom and grow as we reflect back over the things we have learned. Present acts of decision and insight about the past complement each other so that wisdom is accumulated while remaining provisional. Today's insight is always potential fodder for tomorrow's foolishness. Understanding my own life is an existential feedback loop.

The only stable place for an individual to stand, as far as Kierkegaard was concerned, is the eternal life found in Christ. Life in Christ offers the necessary foundation outside of time, even as the believer moves and breathes in time — just as Jesus was the eternal Son of God embracing mortality — where eternity illumines the handful of years we are given in this world. Only death, both daily death to this world and my final exit from this world, will reveal the truth about myself.

What is true of each individual life story is equally true for all history, human and divine. World history happens forward, but historians analyze and write their histories backward. Salvation history moves providentially forward, but the apostles and authors of Holy Scripture perceive and inter-

---

for his own polemical purposes in responding to the concepts of Platonic recollection and Hegelian mediation; see *Repetition* (Princeton: Princeton University Press, 1983) 148-49: "The dialectic of repetition is easy, for that which is repeated has been — otherwise it could not be repeated — but the very fact that it has been makes the repetition something new. . . . When the Greeks said that all knowing is recollecting, they said that all existence, which is, has been; when one says that life is a repetition, one says: actuality, which has been, now comes into existence. If one does not have the category of recollection or of repetition, all life dissolves into empty, meaningless noise."

pret God's plan backward. Interpreting historical experience through the lens of the gospel imagination is every disciple's approach to any genuine understanding of life's meaning, whether peering into the tangles of a troubled marriage or wrestling with the connections between the exodus and Calvary.[67] Whatever a believer considers, be it a personal crisis, the claims of the man from Nazareth, or even the Old Testament hopes for salvation, once a believer has leapt by faith into a new future with Christ, we (believers) are obliged to look back under the direction of this gospel, the good news revealed according to the Scriptures. This gospel message is only properly seen and understood by looking backward while living forward in faith.

67. G. K. Beale and D. A. Carson, eds., *Commentary on the New Testament Use of the Old Testament* (Grand Rapids: Baker, 2007) xxvii defend the perspective on intra-canonical interpretation challenged throughout this chapter by claiming that none of the New Testament authors ever say anything like, "Oh, if only you could experience Jesus Christ the way we do, you would then enjoy a different set of lenses that would enable you to read the Bible differently." However, I believe I have shown that this is, in fact, precisely what the New Testament writers do say, repeatedly.

CHAPTER 3

Offended by Uncertainty

If the rich young man were to give away his possessions because he is bored with them, then his resignation would not amount to much.

Johannes de Silentio/Søren Kierkegaard, *Fear and Trembling*

The previous chapter described the Christian faith as one that orients the Christian life forward and then illuminates backward. The forward leap is personal and subjective; it occurs when an individual embraces Jesus of Nazareth as the Messiah no one expected. The backward illumination then applies this faith perspective to the task of reading Scripture — as well as to the whole of life. It occurs each time this radical trust in Jesus illuminates a reinterpretation of the Old Testament in such a way that Jesus, the Messiah no one expected, is scripturally transfigured into Jesus, the messiah God always intended.

An attentive reader will notice that a crucial question remains unanswered: What could possibly have possessed any of Jesus' contemporaries to make such a leap? Why would the first disciples risk investing all their religious hopes in such an unlikely candidate as Jesus of Nazareth? Explaining this leap of faith is one thing; accounting for the personal motivations that pushed someone over the brink of decision is something else altogether.

Imagine reading a story about a man who jumps from a three-story building as it goes up in flames, landing securely in the firefighters' safety net below. Now imagine coming across a second story about a circus stuntman who jumps nightly from a three-story platform, landing dramatically in a six-foot pool of water. Finally, imagine one last account about a man who deliberately jumps three stories to his death, having recently lost his entire family in an auto accident.

Three different people each make a leap, but their motivations are entirely different, so different in fact that the leaps themselves are incomparable. Though all three experienced the same physical phenomena of aerodynamics, drag, and gravitational pull as their bodies fell through space, their stories, and thus the significance of their leaps, are as different as chalk and cheese. Different motivations stamp each leap as unique. The first jump is lifesaving, the second entertaining, the third tragic. The differences among them arise from motivation. Understanding *what* cannot be separated from knowing *why*. So it is with the leap of faith.

Although the canonical Gospels cannot be expected to provide psychological or motivational analysis of all the players in every story, they do preserve reliable historical traditions concerning the diverse evaluations and decisions made about Jesus by many who encountered him and wrestled with his teaching. The earliest Gospel, Mark, insists that the answer to our motivational question is found in the person of Jesus himself.[1] It was the individual's encounter with Jesus' own audacious exercise of personal spiritual authority that first attracted many and eventually repelled others. This same authority finally convinced the disciples to jump the historical chasm and entrust their religious hopes to the man from Nazareth. Mark highlights the personal effects of both the content of Jesus' teaching and the acts of power that accompanied it:

> The people were amazed at his teaching, because he taught them as one who had authority (Mark 1:22).
> The people were all so amazed that they asked each other, "What is this? A new teaching — and with authority. He even gives orders to evil spirits and they obey him" (1:27).
> This amazed everyone and they praised God, saying, "We have never seen anything like this" (2:12).

---

1. I see no good reason to discount the ancient traditions linking Mark's Gospel with the memories and oral traditions of the apostle Peter; see M. Hengel, *Studies in the Gospel of Mark* (Philadelphia: Fortress, 1985), and *The Four Gospels and the One Gospel of Jesus Christ* (Harrisburg: Trinity, 2000) 1-30, 65-68, 76-96; R. Bauckham, *Jesus and the Eyewitnesses: The Gospels as Eyewitness Testimony* (Grand Rapids: Eerdmans, 2006) 124-27, 155-82, 202-39.

When they heard all he was doing, many people came to him (3:8).

When the Sabbath came, he began to teach in the synagogue, and many who heard him were amazed (6:2).

People were overwhelmed with amazement. "He has done everything well," they said. "He even makes the deaf hear and the dumb speak" (7:37).

The chief priests and the teachers of the law heard this and began looking for a way to kill him, for they feared him because the whole crowd was amazed at his teaching (11:18).

Then Jesus said to them, "Give to Caesar what is Caesar's and to God what is God's." And they were amazed at him (12:17).

Not surprisingly, such collective amazement sometimes translated into individual commitment. Jesus called his disciples, saying, "Come follow me," and they did just that. Their obedience required that they abandon their current circumstances to devote full-time allegiance to his ministry (1:17-18, 20; 2:14; 3:13; 10:28; cf. 10:21).

The audacity of making such absolute claims on the basis of one's own self-understanding could easily be interpreted as a grotesque example of religious hubris. Yet, it is a vital component of Mark's portrait of Jesus, an element highlighted early in his narrative when Jesus asserts his authority to forgive sin and to interpret the terms of Sabbath observance (2:1-12; 2:23–3:6).[2] The specific content of Jesus' teaching and the numerous demonstrations of supernatural power that accompanied his words obviously had a crucial role in shaping the public's response. However, Mark wants his readers to understand that Jesus' words and deeds were the visible and audible signs of the absolute authority of a compelling individual that was sometimes disturbing, frequently offensive, but always compelling. The Jesus of Mark has a presence that alone could conjure the specter of an ineffable, absolute authority. This understanding does not psychologize biblical interpretation, as is sometimes asserted, but gives voice to a self-evident aspect of the gospel story line too often muzzled by modern scientific exe-

---

2. W. Loader, *Jesus' Attitude towards the Law: A Study of the Gospels* (Grand Rapids: Eerdmans, 2002) 28-30, 33-38. With respect to these particular episodes, Loader concludes that Mark "seems to see Jesus as one who, in coming with eschatological authority, effectively replaces the authority of Torah as the absolute court of appeal. . . . The conflict is between Jesus, the new authority, who exercises that authority also to interpret Torah and the stereotyped scribal and Pharisaic interpreters" (38).

gesis.[3] The famous "crisis of decision" that Rudolf Bultmann detected at the heart of the apostolic gospel proclamation actually appeared much earlier, during Jesus' earthly ministry:

> In this crisis of decision, the continuity with the past is accordingly abrogated and the present cannot be understood from the point of view of development — [the individual] knows, not on the basis of any past experience or rational deductions, but directly from the immediate situation.[4]

Bultmann's description of an individual's response to the Christian gospel (something he borrowed from Kierkegaard) is equally descriptive of the way the canonical Gospels demonstrate Jesus' own demand that followers place their trust in him. Faith in Jesus was first elicited by something within the Nazarene himself as encountered in "the immediate situation." It is not possible to segregate the words, deeds, or personality of Jesus one from the other so as to evaluate them in isolation. This is akin to trying to grasp the cultural significance of Elvis Presley's music by analyzing his lyrics alone and ignoring the energy and unprecedented charisma of his stage performances, not to mention his vibrating hips!

Attempting such an existential dissection of Jesus was one of Bultmann's unfortunate errors. Jesus' ministry progressed as an integrated whole, and it was this holistic presence that called for individual decision. Faith then sprung from personal encounter as sparks fly from the collision of steel against flint. The first generation of disciples chose to make their own leap over the particular historical and religious chasms between them and

3. Whether to regard this element of Mark's story to be historically accurate is a separate question. My point is that it is an integral part of any honest reading of the Gospel. Bultmann's insistence that Jesus' "personal qualities" had no part to play in the persuasive power of his message, that his personality only aroused antagonism and had nothing to do with eliciting faith, and that "[i]f he had for some men a certain fascination, this may rather have tended to distract attention from the content of his words, and certainly there is no mention of this in the record" is an excellent illustration of methodological bias positing historical reconstructions that run contrary to the grain of the text; see *Jesus and the Word* (New York: Scribner, 1934) 215.

4. *Jesus and the Word*, 87-88. A more Kierkegaardian statement could hardly be found. Bultmann's book on the historical Jesus implicitly acknowledges his conceptual debt to Kierkegaard by frequently referring to the title of Kierkegaard's early work *Either/Or* (*Jesus and the Word*, 31, 34, 35, 41, 79, 85, 92, 97, 98, 118, 119, 120, 131).

the presence of Jesus. As Jesus became more personally compelling than their historical or religious expectations had been, they became disciples.

One gospel narrative in particular proves to be especially helpful in understanding the dynamics at work when a contemporary was confronted with Jesus: the encounter with the rich man in Mark 10:17-27.[5] While any number of gospel narratives could shed light on the moment of decision to follow or reject Jesus, this conversation is so illuminating because it presents a full-orbed account of faith as immediacy after reflection in a way that can remind us of Kierkegaard's view of faith. Though I am tempted to describe this story as an illustration of the Kierkegaardian account of faith, it would be more precise to say that Kierkegaard's thoroughly biblical understanding of faith is aptly demonstrated in this story. The story reveals faith (or unbelief, in this particular instance) as following or failing to follow due to a personal encounter with Jesus. This encounter provides the occasion to choose between (a) faith or offense, (b) uncertainty or certainty, and (c) becoming an individual or remaining a member of the crowd.

A Good Teacher?

Here I will focus specifically on the personal exchange between Jesus and the rich man.[6] Locating the narrative within Mark's larger literary frame-

---

5. Though Jesus' conversation with this man ends at v. 22, the evaluative remarks in vv. 23-27 will also be helpful to this study. Discussion of various pre-literary possibilities for the traditions in vv. 17-31 may be found in N. Walter, "Zur Analyse von Mc 10.17-31," *Zeitschrift für die Neuetestamentliche Wissenschaft* 53 (1962): 206-18; E. Best, *Disciples and Discipleship: Studies in the Gospel According to Mark* (Edinburgh: Clark, 1986) 17-30; C. Evans, *Mark 8:27–16:20* (Nashville: Nelson, 2001) 91-93; J. Marcus, *Mark 8–16: A New Translation with Introduction and Commentary* (New Haven: Yale University Press, 2009) 724, 734. The evidence that each component of the pericope contains authentic historical tradition is exceedingly strong; see the arguments of V. Taylor, *The Gospel According to St. Mark* (London: Macmillan, 1963) 429-30; M. Hooker, *The Gospel According to Saint Mark* (London: Black, 1991) 241-42; R. Gundry, *Mark: A Commentary on His Apology for the Cross* (Grand Rapids: Eerdmans, 1993) 560; Evans, *Mark 8:27–16:20*, 92-93; Marcus, *Mark 8–16*, 724. For an analysis of the unit's literary structure see C. E. B. Cranfield, *The Gospel According to Saint Mark* (Cambridge: Cambridge University Press, 1959) 325-26; R. Busemann, *Die Jüngergemeinde nach Markus 10. Eine redaktionsgeschichtliche Untersuchung des 10. Kapitels im Markusevangelium* (Bonn: Hanstein, 1983) 15-102; B. Witherington, *The Gospel of Mark: A Socio-Rhetorical Commentary* (Grand Rapids: Eerdmans, 2001) 281.

6. Three questions typically attract the attention of commentators. First, what does the

work (8:22–10:52) is essential for understanding the dramatic effect of both Jesus' startling demand and the rich man's unexpected response.[7] In Mark, genuine disciples are depicted as those who not only recognize Jesus as Messiah (8:27-30) but also answer his call to "follow me" and walk in his path of humiliation, suffering, and death (8:34-38; 9:30-32; 10:32-34). Disciples become subservient like little children and embrace a life of complete obedience to Jesus and service to others (9:33-37; 10:13-16, 31, 43-45). Mark's Jesus insists that the eternal stakes in the decision to become a disciple are so high that it is better to finish one's life maimed and destitute (8:35-37), if that is what faithfulness requires, than to be finally "thrown into hell, where 'their worm does not die, and the fire is not quenched'" (9:43-48). After all, what good is it to accumulate the treasures of this world if they eventually demand your very soul (8:36)?

Furthermore the rich man's approach to Jesus is especially noteworthy. He exhibits a very high level of enthusiasm as the only person reported in the Gospel as falling on his knees after running to greet Jesus and as calling Jesus "Good Teacher." This intense degree of reverence also has no parallels in the Jewish literature of the time apart from one fourth-century rabbinic example.[8] It is also the only narrative in which Jesus is said to have engaged a questioner and "loved him" (v. 21), a detail that heightens the dramatic significance of the loved one's final refusal to follow. Each of these elements in the story's context heightens the emotional contrast framing the story. The somber man who walks away grieving in v. 22 is the polar opposite of the breathless enthusiast racing expectantly toward the Teacher in v. 17. The most likely of all candidates for discipleship exits

---

man intend by calling Jesus "good," and why does Jesus seemingly shirk the commendation? Second, does Jesus accept the man's claim to have kept all the commandments, and what bearing does the law then have on Jesus' view of eternal life? Third, is Jesus' command that the man renounce his wealth and give it all to the poor directed only to him, or is it a universal requirement of every would-be disciple? The focus of this study does not require extensive investigation into these issues.

7. R. Meye, *Jesus and the Twelve: Discipleship and Revelation in Mark's Gospel* (Grand Rapids: Eerdmans, 1968) 73-74, 86; Best, *Disciples*, 2; W. Egger, *Nachfolge als Weg zum Leben. Chancen neuerer exegetischer Methoden dargelegt an Mk 10,17-31* (Klosterneuburg: Österreichisches Katholisches Bibelwerk, 1979) 64.

8. Cranfield, *Gospel According to Saint Mark*, 326; J. Gnilka, *Das Evangelium nach Markus 2* (Cologne: Neukirchener, 1979) 85; Evans, *Mark 8:27–16:20*, 95; A. Yarbro Collins, *Mark: A Commentary* (Minneapolis: Fortress, 2007) 477.

Mark's story line a tragic refusenik who has made the most wrong of all possible wrong decisions. What happened?

The answer to this question is deceptively simple — meeting Jesus happened. Like any good magnet, Jesus can repel as powerfully as he attracts, which is what happens to the rich man once he confronts the demanding reality of Jesus face to face. Knowing about Jesus was no longer a matter of listening to the rumor mill or calculating the Nazarene's reputation from afar; it had become a matter of personal encounter. The rich man soon discovers that Jesus was searching for followers, not admirers; in fact, Jesus' entire ministry was designed in such a way as to make mere admiration impossible.[9] In deflecting the rich man's adulation as he does by questioning his identification of Jesus as a "good teacher" (vv. 18-19), Jesus cleared the air of unhelpful distractions in order to focus the man's attention on the challenge to follow. Then, presuming to know the man's innermost secrets, Jesus commanded him to do something outlandish: "Go, sell everything you have and give to the poor. Then come, follow me" (v. 21).

As if on cue, Jesus' words transform admiration into discouragement. The magnet from Nazareth speaks, reverses polarity, and begins to repel the rich man. The disparity between initial expectations and actual experience creates a situation ripe for disappointment, for the dark hole of personal angst that opens all too easily whenever our expectations go unmet. The greater our expectations, the larger that hole may become. Thus the potential for a letdown is unusually profound when standing face to face with an authority figure we thought possessed enough wisdom to answer life's deepest questions, questions such as "How do I inherit eternal life?" (v. 17).[10] Although Jesus was a beacon that attracted this questioner from a distance, even so the seeker was quickly driven away once the light turned to shine on him.

---

9. See Kierkegaard's biting discussion of the differences between an admirer and a follower of Jesus in *Practice in Christianity* (Princeton: Princeton University Press, 1991) 237-57.

10. There is no reason to assume that the rich man is being insincere or resorting to flattery, contrary to the suggestions of commentators such as D. Nineham, *Saint Mark* (Philadelphia: Westminster, 1963) 270; A. Stock, *The Method and Message of Mark* (Wilmington: Glazier, 1989) 271; J. R. Donahue and D. J. Harrington, *The Gospel of Mark* (Collegeville: Liturgical, 2002) 303. Elsewhere in Mark, when people approach Jesus with ulterior motives, the ruse is plainly identified (10:2; 11:27-33; 12:13-17, 18-27).

The Good Teacher Becomes Offensive

Bowing before Jesus, this man confronts his own moment of decision, a moment that Kierkegaard described as "the occasion."[11] Occasions present themselves whenever we meet a challenge to our current preferred ways of thinking and living. They provide us with opportunities for personal transformation. A self-centered husband is presented such an occasion when his long-suffering wife says over dinner, "I can't live like this anymore; unless something changes, I'm leaving."

How do we respond to the challenges stirred up by someone other than ourselves who confronts us with the unexpected? In this case, the encounter with Jesus became the rich man's definitive occasion challenging his entire way of living, past, present, and future. The story is paradigmatic, for according to Mark, every new encounter with Jesus becomes an opportunity for determining a person's eternal destiny. The rich man had at least asked the most vital question of the most informed source, "What must I do to inherit eternal life?"

When hearing Jesus' response, the rich man has two options. He may respond to Jesus with either faith or offense. For, as Kierkegaard rightly understood, the opposite of faith is not doubt, as is often supposed, but offense. The relationship between faith and offense is a central theme in Kierkegaard; for example, in his treatise on Christian discipleship, *Practice in Christianity,* he writes:

> The possibility of offense is the crossroad, or it is like standing at the crossroad. From the possibility of offense, one turns either to offense or to faith, but one never comes to faith except from the possibility of offense. The possibility of offense, as we have tried to show, is present at every moment, confirming at every moment the chasmic abyss between the single individual and [Jesus] over which faith and faith alone reaches. . . . The possibility of offense is the stumbling block for all, whether they choose to believe or they are offended.[12]

11. See *Philosophical Fragments* (Princeton: Princeton University Press, 1985) 55-71, 99-105.

12. *Practice in Christianity,* 81, 139. For clarity's sake, I have replaced Kierkegaard's "the God-man" (139) with "Jesus" since this is clearly his intended reference.

In the moment of decision, faith and offense are the two poles available for anyone who must choose for or against Jesus. There is no such thing as neutrality when an individual is confronted by Jesus with his invasive, presumptuous, personal demands. If faith were primarily the end product of logical argument, then the reasonable doubt that hovers over insufficient evidence and dubious logic would be faith's legitimate alternative. But exercising faith in Jesus is not explicable by logical principles or the courtroom's rules of evidence. Faith is ultimately attained only by leaping across the chasm.[13] Belief and unbelief are not matters of mental calculation alone but existential concerns engaging the whole person, including the will and the emotions. This was not lost on Kierkegaard who referred to long-term, life-affecting, decision-influencing emotions as "passions."

Thus faith's true alternative does not arise from the failure of reason but from a failure of the will, a failure of passion. Unbelief is evidence of the individual's bondage to personal offense and is therefore an expression of individual sinfulness. Choosing to be ruled by the offensiveness of Jesus' demands, as opposed to trusting him despite his seeming unreasonableness, is finally to choose rebellion against God. Like all examples of sin, Kierkegaardian offense is the expression of an individual's "passionate clinging to autonomy."[14] Thus faith and offense are revealed as opposing passions. Perhaps Christian faith is best described as passionate clinging to Jesus. Unfortunately, the rich man would not be clinging to Jesus anytime soon, for he chose autonomy over discipleship.

Offense and the Individual

The story of the rich man's choosing offense over faith and obedience to Jesus' demand brings at least three issues to the fore for us today: (1) the personal risk involved, (2) the transgression of cultural and religious

13. At different junctures, Kierkegaard refers to both a "leap to faith" and the "leap required for faith"; for a helpful discussion of this ambiguity, see M. J. Ferreira, "Faith and the Kierkegaardian Leap," in *The Cambridge Companion to Kierkegaard* (ed. A. Hannay and G. D. Marino; Cambridge: Cambridge University Press, 1998) 207-32.

14. C. S. Evans, *Faith beyond Reason: A Kierkegaardian Account* (Grand Rapids: Eerdmans, 1998) 106; also see D. J. Gouwens, *Kierkegaard as Religious Thinker* (Cambridge: Cambridge University Press, 1996) 128-33.

norms, and (3) whether an individual like Jesus could wield the authority to dictate the terms of eternal life. We will look at each issue in turn.

The first and most obvious stumbling block has already been mentioned briefly. To say that Jesus asked this man to take a risk is an understatement. In the world of first-century Palestine, abandoning all family and property was an excellent scheme for threatening one's very existence.[15] Material wealth, both ancient and modern, goes a long way toward insulating against the cold hardships of life in a dog-eat-dog world, especially in an agrarian, hierarchical, limited-goods society like first-century Palestine. In simple human terms, it was entirely reasonable, even responsible, for this man to ponder long and hard before doing what Jesus asked.[16] As a wise man once said, money can't buy happiness, but it can make a sizeable down payment. When someone stands up and says to a crowd, "Give away everything you own and throw in your lot with me!" he shouldn't be surprised if members of the audience first ask for a résumé and a long, *long*-range business plan. Jesus offers neither of these things, but expects on-the-spot obedience nonetheless. How many professing Christians today in fact secretly sympathize with the rich man's hesitation? How many would offer Jesus their financial advice rather than obey such a radical call?

Second, following Jesus would have entailed transgressing a number of cultural and religious norms, requiring a radical redefinition of the man's self-understanding, his place in society, and his relationship to God. Doing what Jesus asked would require him to behave so idiosyncratically that his life would forever be at odds with every aspect of his upbringing. Jesus' challenge "ran counter to all that he had learned from childhood on the material rewards of piety."[17] Jesus may as well have commanded an ostrich to jump off a cliff, spread its stubby wings, and believe it could fly.

Second Temple Judaism entertained several competing theological explanations for the moral and spiritual conundrums raised by wealth and poverty. On one hand, wealth could be understood as a divine blessing and

---

15. Witherington, *Gospel of Mark*, 284.

16. In this way the rich man also illustrates another of Kierkegaard's favorite themes: reflection alone never produces faith. No amount of evidence, thought, or analysis would have made the required leap of faith any easier.

17. J. Schmid, *The Gospel According to Mark* (New York: Mercier, 1968) 192; see pp. 193-95 for a good summary of the Old Testament evidence and the diverse Jewish attitudes about material possessions current in the time of Jesus.

confirmation of personal piety. In this scheme, poverty was the result of laziness or impiety (almost certainly the view embraced by the rich). On the other hand, abundant wealth could be seen as evidence of one's indifference to and/or exploitation of the poor, while poverty was a sign of piety and a possible means of divine purification (probably the view preferred by most poor people).[18] When Jesus told this man to take a vow of poverty in his quest for eternal life, he made an unprecedented demand unlike anything the man had heard before.[19] The shock value of Jesus' words was certainly intensified by the family upheaval and subsequent social dislocation that would have rippled through the entire community once this landowner had abandoned his home, his real estate, and the numerous tenant workers dependent on his estate for their livelihoods.[20]

18. Some commentators suggest that Jesus assumed the rich man was guilty of similar misbehavior when he replaced the commandment "do not covet" with "do not defraud" (v. 19), intimating that the man had acquired his wealth fraudulently; see Hooker, *Mark,* 241; Gundry, *Mark,* 554; Yarbro Collins, *Mark,* 478; J. Marcus, *Mark 8–16* (New Haven: Yale University Press, 2009) 727. It is an interesting speculation, but nothing more.

19. The rabbis actually forbade giving away all of one's property (Mishnah *Arakkin* 8:4; Babylonian Talmud *Ketuboth* 50a), a tradition that may well reflect a Pharisaic strain of teaching dating back to the first century. Best, *Disciples,* 26, argues that this teaching on poverty must originate with Jesus, since there are no known parallels in Palestinian Judaism.

20. See the historical and social-scientific analyses provided by G. Theissen, "'Wir haben alles verlassen' (Mc. X 28). Nachfolge und soziale Entwurzelung in der jüdisch-palästinischen Gesellschaft des I. Jahrhunderts n. Ch.," *Novum Testamentum* 19 (1977): 161-96; D. May, "Leaving and Receiving: A Social-Scientific Exegesis of Mark 10:29-31," *Perspectives on Religious Studies* 17 (1990): 141-51, 154; J. Hellerman, "Wealth and Sacrifice in Early Christianity: Revisiting Mark's Presentation of Jesus' Encounter with the Rich Young Ruler," *Trinity Journal* 21 (2000): 143-64. Hellerman argues that Jesus intended the "poor" recipients of the rich man's wealth to be the community of disciples, reading the communal existence described in Acts (2:44-46; 4:32-37; 6:1-4) as the continuation of a lifestyle initiated by Jesus. Thus gospel exhortations to "give to the poor" are not calls to almsgiving, as traditionally conceived, but expressions of the Christian ethic to care for one's brothers and sisters. "'Leaving all and following Jesus' meant to view one's material possessions as belonging to the local Christian family as a whole" (164). There are several problems with this suggestion: (1) it is unclear in differentiating the *Sitz im Leben Jesu* and the *Sitz im Leben Ekklesia;* (2) laying up "treasure in heaven" as it appears in the Gospels was a common Jewish idiom for almsgiving; (3) Mark 10 offers no textual indicators that Jesus intended Peter or the other disciples to be identified as the poor; (4) the early church did not limit its generosity to its own members; (5) there is no indication that Peter's claim to have "left all" describes such a transfer of goods; (6) there is no evidence that the model of Acts became a universal expectation; (7) no rationale is given for linking Jesus' demand in Mark 10 with the Jerusalem community in Acts.

A lifetime of conformity to the prevailing social norms naturally predisposed the rich man to reject Jesus' order out of hand. From Mark's perspective, however, Jesus' bizarre instructions are intended to throw cold water over any assumption, natural or unnatural, that simply affirms the inherent privilege presumed by prevailing social and religious customs. This is not the only time Jesus demands something that requires a would-be follower to run roughshod over convention. Jesus is also recorded telling prospective disciples that they must leave their dead unburied (Luke 8:21-22), hate father and mother if they wish to follow him (Luke 14:26), and even make themselves eunuchs for the kingdom of God (Matt. 19:10-12). In making such demands Jesus is not necessarily critiquing convention per se, but he does require a willingness from every follower to break decisively with cultural expectations, not necessarily because the expectations are wrong but simply because Jesus calls all persons to put him and his kingdom above all. The demand of faith, for *this* man, right *now*, is what is at stake. As Kierkegaard puts it, "To have faith is to venture out as decisively as possible for a human being, breaking with everything, with what a human being naturally loves, breaking, in order to save his life, with that in which he naturally has his life."[21]

In this respect, Jesus' word to this man is reminiscent of God's command to Abraham in Genesis 22:2, when the patriarch is told to sacrifice his son Isaac. Both Abraham and the rich man are asked to step beyond the boundaries of socially acceptable behavior. Both stories illustrate vividly the moral and spiritual dilemma famously described by Kierkegaard as the "teleological suspension of the ethical." Is there a higher end or greater goal for which we might properly suspend our normal ethical duties? Both men are asked to forfeit the moral estimate of their peers in order to follow divine instructions.[22] Will they obey the command even though doing so

---

21. *The Moment and Late Writings* (Princeton: Princeton University Press, 1998) 214.

22. See Kierkegaard's *Fear and Trembling,* especially "Problema I: Is There a Teleological Suspension of the Ethical?" and "Problema II: Is There an Absolute Duty to God?" Discussing the many complexities of Kierkegaard's most widely read book is beyond the scope of this study (and the author's ability). For an excellent introduction to the many issues involved, see C. S. Evans and S. Walsh, eds., *Fear and Trembling* (Cambridge: Cambridge University Press, 2006) vi-xxx; also R. Perkins, ed., *Kierkegaard's* Fear and Trembling: *Critical Appraisals* (University: University of Alabama Press, 1981); E. Mooney, *Knights of Faith and Resignation: Reading Kierkegaard's* Fear and Trembling (Albany: State University of New York, 1991); R. Perkins, ed., *International Kierkegaard Commentary:* Fear and Trembling *and*

will make them lawbreakers and social misfits? Genesis 22 and Mark 10 are equally clear: anyone hoping to hear the word of God must be willing to transgress conventional standards, since God is not bound to anyone's conventions.

Such a leap of faith, especially when it is a leap into social unacceptability, moves one *away* from the crowd's preexisting expectations and simultaneously *toward* a new situation of becoming a believing individual.[23] Faith creates a personal relationship. It is not a social contract. In this sense, faith is analogous to death. The Grim Reaper confronts each individual face to face; even the mass tragedy of complete extinction occurs through the death of each and every individual in a species. Just as no one can take someone else's place and face biological death for another, so no one can take the leap of faith and believe for another. Luther's insight into the solitude of dying is an apt description of Christian faith. "Every one must fight his own battle with death by himself, alone . . . for I will not be with you then, nor you with me."[24] Regardless of the environment, whether it is composed of supportive co-religionists or antagonistic cynics, none can take the leap for any but themselves.

Christian faith is an either-or, an all or nothing, a yes or no to God right now. It is based on a decision that can only be rendered by the single individual and is not a collective act. Such passionate, individualized commitment to Jesus does not flourish under the homogenizing regimen of popular opinion. Rather, such passion is typically drowned out by the monotonous voice of the crowd. The collective tends to insist with the persis-

---

Repetition (Macon: Mercer University Press, 1993); J. Lippitt, *Kierkegaard and* Fear and Trembling (London: Routledge, 2003).

23. Kierkegaard's concern for the individual has earned accusations that he promotes an excessive individualism. While aspects of his later writings in particular are subject to this criticism, I personally find this common charge overdrawn. His understanding of human personhood is highly relational and interpersonal: read his principle ethical treatise, *Works of Love* (Princeton: Princeton University Press, 1995), as one example. Also see his own account of why he focused on the individual in "The Individual, Two 'Notes' Concerning My Work as an Author," in *The Point of View for My Work as an Author: A Report to History* (New York: Harper, 1962); also his extensive contrast between life as a member of the crowd and choosing to live as a single individual in *A Literary Review* (London: Penguin, 2006) 53-101.

24. Martin Luther, "Eight Sermons at Wittenberg, 1522," trans. J. Doberstine in *Luther's Works*, vol. 51 (Philadelphia: Fortress, 1980) 70; quoted in S. McGrath, *Heidegger: A (Very) Critical Introduction* (Grand Rapids: Eerdmans, 2008) 54.

tence of a rabid rat-terrier that all community members obligingly submit to convention. But faith requires that we part company with the crowd, trusting that an absolute relationship with Jesus is more important than a relative relationship with the relatives. The rich man was challenged to step out for himself, to act, to choose, to believe individually as an individual — regardless of the offense inevitably created for others (including significant others) in his life. In the end, it was a call he would not obey, and so he stepped away from Jesus and melted again into the crowd.

Offense over *the* Individual

The third aspect of the offense confronting the rich man appeared in the Nazarene himself. Jesus unabashedly puts himself center-stage in his teaching. By what authority did a carpenter from Nazareth dare to redefine the terms of eternal life? Initially, at least, Jesus answered the man's question as any good prophet might, by referring his questioner back to the gracious gift of God's law, "You know the commandments" (10:19).[25] But Jesus then threw a monkey wrench into the conversation. He first took liberties in reciting the second table of the Decalogue by turning the final commandment against "coveting" into an idiosyncratic warning not to "defraud."[26] Perhaps Jesus' rephrasing was an example of midrash, the sort

25. Commentators have aptly noted the strangeness of the rich man's question, for any Jew would have known the correct answer: life is enjoyed by those who keep covenant with the Lord by obeying Torah (Deut. 30:15-16; Lev. 18:5). We can only speculate as to what motivated this man to ask for something more; see Nineham, *Mark,* 270; Schmid, *Mark,* 190. In addition, this exchange regarding obedience to the law has nothing to do with the Pauline debate over whether one is justified by works or by grace, *pace* W. Harnisch, "Die Berufung des Reichen. Zur Analyse von Markus 10, 17-27," in *Festschrift für Ernst Fuchs* (ed. G. Ebeling, E. Jüngel, and G. Schunack; Tübingen: Mohr, 1973) 171-75; J. Degenhardt, "Was muß ich tun, um das ewige Leben zu gewinnen? Zu Mk 10,17-22," in *Biblische Rand bemerkungen* (ed. H. Merklein and J. Lange; Ausburg: Werner Blasaditsch, 1974) 162-66. The rich man's confidence in his Torah observance is presented as a response perfectly acceptable to Jesus, and it is echoed by the apostle Paul himself: "In regard to the law, (I was) a Pharisee . . . as for legalistic righteousness, (I was) faultless" (Phil. 3:5-6); see Schmid, *Mark,* 190-91; R. T. France, *The Gospel of Mark: A Commentary on the Greek Text* (Grand Rapids: Eerdmans, 2002) 401-3.

26. Commentators sometimes suggest that Jesus applied the tenth commandment specifically to the rich man, implying that fraud is a special temptation for the wealthy. Whether or not this is true, Jesus' demeanor in vv. 19-21 gives no indication that Jesus saw this as the man's problem; see Hooker, *Mark,* 241; Collins, *Mark,* 478.

of expository application and commentary that a faithful first-century teacher or even a prophet might perform. However, in the context of Mark's Gospel Jesus' ad hoc rewording of the commandment portrays a Jesus who does not hesitate to act solely on the basis of his own authority.

Jesus' midrash on the Decalogue paves the way for his final answer to the rich man's question. Eternal life comes only to those who obey and follow him (v. 21). This climactic call to surrender is startling, not only because Jesus expresses a view of wealth and poverty unparalleled in his day[27] and not only because he expects the man to abandon his socially acceptable (and divinely allotted?) place in the world, but because he clearly says that the rich man's individual response *to him* will determine his eternal destiny. Jesus the prophet could offer midrash on Torah, calling his listeners to repentance and covenant obedience, but no true prophet would make individual allegiance to himself the criterion for eternal life. At this point, Jesus was no longer prophetic, pious, or midrashic. He became unbelievable, unless, of course, the listener or reader is willing to believe the unbelievable, to throw in their lot with the Messiah no one expected.

Ironically, this was the leap that Rudolf Bultmann, one of the leading twentieth-century theological interpreters of Kierkegaard, some would say misinterpreter, was never willing to make. Bultmann famously insisted that Jesus' proclamation was the presupposition, not the substance, of New Testament theology. Jesus proclaimed the coming of the kingdom, but it was left to the later church to announce the coming of Christ. According to Bultmann's catchy aphorism, "The proclaimer became the proclaimed."[28] Unfortunately, Bultmann's widely accepted thesis either explained away or simply ignored anything in the Gospels that proved inconvenient to his preferred conclusion.

His handling of Mark 10:17-31 in his pioneering volume on form criticism, *History of the Synoptic Tradition,* is a good example of such neglect. Here Bultmann categorizes the entire pericope, or section, as an apophthegm, a cryptic story of doubtful historical value. He maintains this even though he admits that it probably contains isolated sayings going back to Jesus.[29] But the pivotal words in Mark 10:21, together with the par-

27. Best, *Disciples,* 26; Witherington, *Mark,* 283.

28. *Theology of the New Testament* (New York: Scribner, 1951) 1:33.

29. When a saying of Jesus is set within an appropriately constructed narrative framework, created by either the church tradition or the Gospel author, the resulting story is called an apophthegm. At least this is the definition used by form critics such as Bultmann.

allels in Matthew 19:21 and Luke 18:22, are ignored throughout an otherwise painstakingly minute examination of Synoptic traditions.[30] Similarly, his study of the life of Jesus makes no mention of v. 21 specifically and reduces the lesson of vv. 17-22 to an amorphous challenge from Jesus to "do what is right, what everyone knows."[31] The explanation for Bultmann's oversight is not hard to find since the words of Mark 10:21 ("You lack one thing . . . come follow me") stand as an insurmountable obstacle to his theory about the historical Jesus and the nature of the gospel. Not only did Jesus fail to satisfy traditional Jewish expectations of messiahship, as Bultmann also recognized,[32] but Jesus made himself, his teaching, and his personal authority central to the unconventional messiahship unfolding in his earthly ministry. The proclaimer was indeed busy proclaiming himself.

One Thing Is Lacking

Having examined the multiple levels of offense standing in opposition to the rich man's exercise of faith in Jesus, we still need clearly to identify what Jesus was asking the man to do. Whatever the unspoken spiritual vacuum driving this man to search for something more, Jesus addresses his quest for eternal life in the words of v. 21: "You lack one thing. Go, sell everything you have and give to the poor, and you will have treasure in heaven.[33] Then come, follow me." Several issues need to be disentangled at this point.

---

30. R. Bultmann, *History of the Synoptic Tradition* (trans. J. Marsh; New York: Harper, 1963, revised) 54-55. The "Index of Passages" provides no listing for Matt. 19:21; Mark 10:21; or Luke 18:22. Neither are these texts mentioned when their larger pericopae are discussed.

31. *Jesus and the Word,* 97.

32. Bultmann understood this historical point very clearly; see his *Theology,* 1:27: "*Jesus' life and work* measured by traditional messianic ideas *was not messianic.*"

33. Possessing treasure in heaven (v. 21e) is not synonymous with inheriting eternal life (v. 17), so renouncing all his wealth should not be taken as "the one thing" (v. 21b) the rich man lacked for his salvation. "Treasure in heaven" was a technical term for, among other things, God's reward for almsgiving (Matt. 6:19-21; Luke 12:32-34; 1 Tim. 6:17-19). The promise of heavenly treasure is the result of "giving to the poor" (v. 21d), not "selling everything you have" (v. 21c). Neither Second Temple Judaism nor the New Testament knows anything about heavenly blessing for ascetic renunciation in itself. Jesus' promise of divine blessing for the rich man's almsgiving accords with the tacit acceptance of the man's claim to Torah observance in vv. 19-20.

First, we should note that Jesus actually tells the man to do two things — sell your possessions and follow me — after diagnosing his problem as the absence of one thing. Are we to understand both actions combined as the one thing still lacking? If so, what is the relationship between the renunciation of material goods and following Jesus?

Second, the rich man's unexplained dissatisfaction with his religious tradition is addressed in a demand for actions that have nothing to do with the dictates of Torah. How are we to understand, then, the relationship between the "one thing" and the rich man's claim to have kept the law faithfully all his life?

Various answers to these questions are offered by commentators. They can be categorized under two headings: command interpretations and corrective interpretations. The command interpretations of Jesus' words view the "one thing lacking" in a positive sense, as a new departure, a new requirement, something yet to be performed that will prove decisive for the rich man's future.[34] The corrective interpretations on the other hand view the "one thing lacking" negatively, as a characteristic shortfall in the man's behavior that Jesus now challenges him to correct.

Command interpretations of v. 21 typically draw attention to one or both of Jesus' injunctions (give to the poor and follow me) and the need for an immediate response. Some interpreters single out the act of monetary renunciation as the "one thing lacking."[35] For a few, this is a call to radical asceticism and a hallmark of a decisively new Christian ethic.[36] However, most interpreters in this group read Jesus' two commands in conjunction with each other. Obeying the call to renunciation becomes the visible demonstration of uncompromising devotion to God, the type of devotion required in order to truly follow Jesus.[37]

34. Whether the one thing lacking is "one more" thing or "the only" thing cannot be adjudicated by lexicography alone. Commentators who address this question typically settle on the second option of "the only"; for further discussion, see Gundry, *Mark*, 554; W. Schmithals, *Das Evangelium nach Markus* (Gütersloh: Gütersloher Verlagshaus Mohn, 1979) 453-54.

35. France, *Mark*, 403; Donahue and Harrington, *Mark*, 306.

36. For Donahue and Harrington, *Mark*, 306-7, Jesus' command is radical because he requires disciples to make a vow of poverty; for Witherington, *Mark*, 283, Jesus' call to renunciation shows that he requires more than mere "law keeping": he expects "faultlessness." Jesus raises the bar for godliness by defining "a new Jewish ethic." Ironically, Gundry, *Mark*, 554, sees Jesus' demands as an implied criticism of salvation through obedience to Torah.

37. Taylor, *Mark*, 429; Evans, *Mark 8:27–16:20*, 99; Schmithals, *Das Evangelium*, 453-54; Schmid, *Mark*, 191; Marcus, *Mark*, 728.

Corrective interpreters assume that Jesus possessed special insight into the rich man's personality and past religious devotion. For these commentators, Jesus' charge that the man give everything to the poor arose from this special insight. The command is therefore a remedial measure intended to correct the rich man's past failures. Though commentators differ as to what his sins may include, all agree that his excessive wealth was a visible sign of his corruption.[38] However, Jesus' conversation with the rich man offers no evidence of insincerity on either man's part. There is nothing in the text that justifies the assumption that Jesus was trying to redress a moral flaw that had contributed to making this man rich. Even though some commentators combine the corrective and command interpretations, the highly speculative nature of the corrective readings in my view decisively favors seeing Jesus' words as a command.

It is also important to distinguish two distinct concerns in the text that corrective interpreters typically confuse. First, the rich man's past devotion to God should not be conflated with his current decision not to follow Jesus. If the rich man abandoned all of his wealth, would it be a testimony to his prior life of piety or evidence of his current submission to Jesus' authority? For Christian readers, it is all too easy to collapse these two issues into one, automatically assuming that the man's response to Jesus reveals his prior relationship to God.[39] On this reading of the story, clinging to his wealth belies the man's claim to obedient Torah observance. Rejecting Jesus would thus reveal him to be on less familiar terms with God than he imagined.

But following this line of reasoning produces a pious anachronism. The suggestion that the rich young man's refusal of Jesus' call to absolute renunciation is in any way symptomatic of a character flaw or a religious shortcoming is simply not supported by the text. This is true even if we attribute amazing insight to Jesus; such a reading is itself a faith-based conclusion not supported by the evidence. Given the Gospel author's own location and time, he could never have assumed that his original readers

38. Explanations as to how the man's wealth demonstrates his personal and/or spiritual failure include: he lacks concern for the poor (Evans, *Mark 8:27–16:20*, 98), he is self-interested and devoid of genuine devotion to God (Hooker, *Mark*, 242; Schmithals, *Das Evangelium*, 454), money has become his idol (Cranfield, *Mark*, 330), and he lacks the (Greco-Roman) ideal of self-mastery (Yarbro Collins, *Mark*, 479).

39. Schmithals, *Das Evangelium*, 453-54; Hooker, *Mark*, 242; Cranfield, *Mark*, 330 all provide examples of this conflation.

would interpret obedience to Jesus as an act of Jewish piety. Quite the opposite! Furthermore, Jesus' loving response to the man's self-confident assertion of life-long Torah observance indicates that Jesus accepted his claim at face value. His hunger for eternal life had nothing to do with any failure to observe God's gift of Torah. His eventual refusal to follow Jesus does not require us to conclude that he came to Jesus as a religious hypocrite. Jesus' question about the Decalogue was not intended to answer the man's question about eternal life. For whatever reason, Jesus was content not to plumb the unspoken motivation behind this man's quest. Instead, by raising the issue of Torah, Jesus accomplishes two important, personal transactions with his conversation partner. First, he affirms the religious heritage held in common by both of them. Second, this shared religious affirmation supports the Old Testament covenant that is at the root of Jesus' command. Although Jesus and his message of the kingdom are a new spiritual reality that confronts this man, they still emerge out of the Old Testament heritage.

The rich man must confront his own moment of decision. There is no reason to assume that this anxious questioner now standing nose to nose with the demanding preacher from Nazareth should have equated obedience to Jesus with the performance of a *mitzvah* or a command from his beloved Torah. Why should he have seen following Jesus as an act of covenant obedience? There was no self-evident reason for him to have drawn such a conclusion. A life of Torah obedience had led him to ask Jesus a pressing question, but it did not lead him to understand why he should now surrender control over his life to this man from Galilee.

That is the point. Jesus' call to renunciation was not intended as a measure of the rich man's piety, at least not in the way that many suggest. Jesus was not testing the depths of his love for Yahweh or the stringency of his adherence to Torah.[40] Rather, the question now confronting this man was not whether he had been faithful to the commandments but *whether he would become faithful to Jesus.*[41] Whether following Jesus and doing

40. Vv. 22-25 identify the man's character flaw and the pivotal role materialism played in his rejection of Jesus, but that insight is the fruit of Jesus' later reflection and Markan commentary; it does not arise from the preceding conversation. These observations in no way diminish the crucial role of Jesus' ominous warnings about the inherent spiritually destructive power of wealth in vv. 23-25.

41. I disagree with those, such as Loader, *Jesus' Attitude,* 92 and Yarbro Collins, *Mark,* 479, who conclude that Jesus endorses Torah obedience as remaining sufficient for the in-

what Jesus requires demonstrates commitment to Yahweh is entirely *a question of faith* — the very thing this man refused to exercise. Was he willing to make a leap, a new beginning? Would he grant this man from Nazareth a totally unanticipated level of authority over his life? By turning away from Jesus as he did, the man who initially seemed so eager to believe sadly reveals his preference for personal offense. Thus as he turns to leave Mark's stage, the curtain falls on any and all future claims to true devotion for this rich man. Jesus' demand introduces a sharp note of historical and personal discontinuity into this man's life story.

The supposition of the corrective interpreters discussed above that the rich man's response to Jesus was somehow predictable, foreseeable, or at least consistent with some hidden truth about the man's past now revealed by Jesus just doesn't hold up. In reading this passage, we should do nothing to dull the sharp edges of the profound uncertainties, personal, historical, and religious, that in the face of Jesus stare this man in the face. By enhancing Jesus' prophetic gravitas, crediting him with an insight that is nowhere suggested in the text, Christian interpreters effectively undercut the key ingredient of suspense lying at the heart of the story. The result, however unintended, becomes another seductive attempt at building bridges where only a leap will do. The rich man kneeled before another devout son of Abraham who called him to make a completely unforeseen, unanticipated leap into uncertainty — a leap both continuous yet discontinuous with everything in his past.

In matters of faith, such uncertainty is unavoidable. Uncertainty is inherent to every leap of faith. Wanting faith without uncertainty is like asking for a surprise party and expecting to sit on the planning committee. The only solution to the objective uncertainty that makes faith necessary is the personal certitude created by the act of believing. This is the irreducible paradox lurking at the heart of Christian faith. Without uncertainty there is no reason to believe, for then we would know, and there would be no risk in believing.[42] But when an individual risks believing in the face of

---

heritance of eternal life. Jesus is certainly a faithful Jew who observes the commandments himself, just as he readily accepts this man's evaluation of his own past devotion. But the matter of inheriting eternal life is addressed in v. 21, when Jesus authoritatively adds a new command all his own.

42. Religious apologists who respond by insisting that faith is another way of knowing miss the point and remain confused about the nature of religious belief. As Kierkegaard explains in *Concluding Unscientific Postscript to Philosophical Fragments I* (Princeton: Prince-

such uncertainty, faith gives birth to its own personal certitude. Faith after the fact becomes its own confirmation. By demanding certainty in advance we submerge even the possibility of faith. This defense of uncertainty is not a ploy to turn ignorance into a virtue; it simply intends to clarify that, in relation to Jesus, complete certainty is never possible. Could the rich man ever know *with certainty* that following Jesus would necessarily lead him to eternal life?

Kierkegaard's frequent comparison of faith with swimming the ocean's depths captures the essential relationship between faith and uncertainty. If we demand certainty in our lives, then we'd best remain standing on dry land. But, please, do not pretend that lying on the ground and flailing both arms in circles has anything to do with swimming.

> The believer continually lies out on the deep, has 70,000 fathoms of water beneath him. However long he lies out there, this still does not mean that he will gradually end up lying and relaxing onshore. He can become more calm, more experienced, find a confidence that loves jest and a cheerful temperament — but until the very last he lies out on 70,000 fathoms of water.[43]

Faith may expand; it may grow more assured, more comfortable, and more familiar over time, just as an experienced swimmer grows more competent

---

ton University Press, 1992) 29: "Faith does not result from straightforward scholarly deliberation, nor does it come directly; on the contrary, in this objectivity one loses that infinite, personal, impassioned interestedness, which is the condition of faith . . . in this certainty that lurks at faith's door and craves for it, [the believer] is rather in such a precarious position that much effort, much fear and trembling will be needed lest he fall into temptation and confuse knowledge with faith. Whereas up to now faith has had a beneficial taskmaster in uncertainty, it would have its worst enemy in this certainty. That is, if passion is taken away, faith no longer exists, and certainty and passion do not hitch up as a team."

43. *Stages on Life's Way: Studies by Various Persons* (Princeton: Princeton University Press, 1988) 444. Kierkegaard often returns to the idea of faith as floating over "seventy thousand fathoms"; for instance, see *Postscript,* 204: "Without risk, no faith. Faith is the contradiction between the infinite passion of inwardness and the objective uncertainty. If I am able to apprehend God objectively, I do not have faith; but because I cannot do this, I must have faith. If I want to keep myself in faith, I must continually see to it that I hold fast the objective uncertainty, see to it that in the objective uncertainty I am 'out on 70,000 fathoms of water' and still have faith." For a good discussion of the paradoxical relationship between faith and (un)certainty, see J. H. Thomas, *Subjectivity and Paradox: A Study of Kierkegaard* (Oxford: Blackwell, 1957) 45-76.

in kicking and pulling at the water, but the true believer never manages to touch bottom, not even on tip-toe. Once we find ourselves standing, we know that we have stopped swimming.

This unavoidable, individual plunge into 70,000 fathoms of uncertainty also provides the important answer to an apparent contradiction appearing in Mark 10:23-27.[44] On the one hand, Jesus declares that it is impossible for the man to be saved. After all, he holds out more hope for a camel contortionist wiggling through a needle's eye than he does for this rich man entering into eternal life (vv. 23-25).[45] On the other hand, when the shocked disciples, who obviously share the popular assumption that wealth is a sign of divine blessing, object to Jesus' verdict (if this man can't get into the kingdom, then what chance do we have?), Jesus quickly assures them that "all things are possible with God" (vv. 26-27). But which is it? Some interpreters have suggested that the tension serves to clarify the priority of God's grace, highlighting that salvation is always the gift of God and never a human achievement.[46] While this suggestion is helpful, it finally fails to resolve the problem, for an important question remains: If the God of grace can do anything, why did he not make it possible for this particular rich man to experience new life in the kingdom? Did Jesus issue a check that the Father refused to endorse?

Fortunately, Mark never suggests that Jesus might take back with one hand what he offers in the other. All his transactions are honest and above-board. He provided this man with a genuine occasion for faith; had he chosen to obey, Jesus would never have withdrawn the opportunity to follow him. Yet one thing God cannot do is create an occasion for faith devoid of uncertainty. This is as much an oxymoron as asking the Creator to shape a square circle or to draw a three-sided rectangle. The uncertainty of faith confronts each individual as a chasm, never a bridge or a thoroughfare, but always as a stark, open chasm waiting to be jumped. Whatever

44. Source and tradition critics often point to this contradiction as evidence of Mark's association of originally independent traditions; see Walter, "Zur Analyse," 210. Whether or not this is the case, the apparent contradiction between Jesus' assertions in vv. 23-25 and what he says in v. 27 is an unavoidable part of Mark's final composition. Interpreting the final form of Mark's narrative requires moving beyond appeals to pre-Markan tradition.

45. Modern commentators agree that Jesus' colorful metaphor is intended to denote the impossible; see Marcus, *Mark*, 731.

46. For instance, see Harnisch, "Die Berufung," 173-74; Degenhardt, "Was muß ich tun," 165-66.

God may have made possible for the rich man, the man remained responsible to embrace the uncertainty and to leap for himself.

Faith, Past and Present

Jesus' ministry drew a stark line in the sands of sacred history. The way to eternal life appears in obedience to his call; stepping over this line is the one thing now necessary. His authoritative proclamation of the Good News inaugurated the New Covenant, in which he became the measure of all present and future devotion. For Jesus not only wields authority to offer unique commentary on and application of the Decalogue, his words confront the rich man, as well as Mark's readers, in effect, as the new law. While this is not the place to explore what one scholar aptly describes as "the enigmatic nature of Jesus' relationship to the Mosaic Law,"[47] it is clear that Mark believes Torah-obedience has been thoroughly modified, perhaps even rescinded, in the gospel call to Christian discipleship. Jesus is not radicalizing the law; he is surpassing it altogether by his personal presence and all-embracing demands. In the words of William Loader, "Jesus declares his own Torah."[48] The offensiveness of the gospel did not wait for the cross at Calvary (1 Cor. 1:18-25); it rose up boldly in Jesus' own lifetime. This offense stands ready to grab Mark's readers by the scruff of the neck as Jesus presumes to add a new and final commandment to the faith of Abraham, Moses, and Isaiah: follow me.

The pivotal lesson of Mark 10:17-22 is that faith reveals an individual's relationship to God moment by moment in an ever present immediacy. Consequently, the obedience of faith never rests on its laurels. Past devotion is only as personally significant as the present act of faith and obedience. Here is the truth that Kierkegaard refers to when he talks about the immediacy of faith. Immediacy is the "here and nowness" of believing in Jesus. The immediacy after reflection is the commitment and continual

47. J. P. Meier, *A Marginal Jew: Rethinking the Historical Jesus 4: Law and Love* (New Haven: Yale University Press, 2009) 297.

48. *Jesus' Attitude*, 91; also see R. Banks, *Jesus and the Law in the Synoptic Tradition* (Cambridge: Cambridge University Press, 1975) 163-64. Though I agree with Loader's insights into Mark's emphasis on Jesus' personal authority (92), his agreement with those who read Jesus' command as a criticism of the man's religious past and an affirmation of the adequacy of Torah observance for eternal life is, I believe, a weakness in his analysis.

recommitment made on due consideration of Christ's daily demands. The common Christian temptation to suggest that the rich man's failure to believe insinuates something faulty about his prior relationship with God is not hard to understand. After all, someone who already believes in Jesus can easily imagine that true devotion should have prepared this man to respond faithfully once he heard the Messiah's voice. The Gospel of John will pick up this theological thread and make a strong argument in favor of faith's retrospective ability to reinterpret an individual's past (see chapter 5 below). We have already examined the power of Christian faith to reinterpret the Old Testament in light of its fulfillment (chapter 2), but the reinterpretation of a person's past by faith is a theological idea not found in Mark's Gospel.[49]

The lesson of Mark's rich man is that the unusual prophet from Nazareth confronts each individual afresh, regardless of past devotion or present understanding. He calls each of us to choose, here and now. Jesus' demands set off a spiritual earthquake, leaving a sizeable crevasse separating personal expectation from divine command. The rich young man found himself at this chasm, caught completely by surprise. He never expected to lurch precariously at the existential edge as he anxiously sought Jesus that day. But neither had he anticipated the challenge of a homeless ex-carpenter who dared to define eternal life in the first person. When the moment of decision arrived, the man chose to walk away on dry land rather than to take the plunge with Jesus into the 70,000 fathoms of faithful uncertainty.

---

49. In this respect, Mark's theology of the covenant is reminiscent of Paul's description of the law in Gal. 3:24-25: "The law was put in charge until Christ came that we might be justified by faith. Now that faith has come, we are no longer under the supervision of the law" (NIV). Concerning other religious leaders in Mark, the teacher of the law described in Mark 12:28-34 is somewhat reminiscent of the rich man in that Jesus concludes that he is "not far from the kingdom" (v. 34). Otherwise, Jesus accused Pharisees and teachers of the law of hypocrisy, either explicitly (7:1-16; 12:38-40) or implicitly (8:11-13); he also accused a group of Sadducees of not knowing Scripture or the power of God (12:24).

CHAPTER 4

The Apostle Paul, from Encounter to Belief

In the proclamation, Christ himself, indeed God himself, encounters the hearer, and the "Now" in which the preached word sounds forth is the "Now" of the eschatological occurrence itself.

Bultmann, *Theology of the New Testament*

In turning to the life of Paul and his famous experience on the road to Damascus, this chapter will move from the first to the second generation of Jesus' followers. Paul, perhaps the last apostle, receives his call in such an extraordinary way that he refers to himself as a "miscarriage" (1 Cor. 15:8). He is a transitional figure between the two generations, the eyewitnesses to Jesus' life on earth and those who came after. We do not know if Paul ever heard or saw Jesus himself, but he was a contemporary of Jesus who initially rejected any claim that Jesus could have been the Messiah. Paul's later announcements of a revelatory encounter with the ascended, glorified Jesus set him on a path to becoming the apostle to the Gentiles. He would proclaim the message of a Jewish Messiah to Greco-Roman audiences who had never seen or heard Jesus for themselves. The various dynamics at work in this historical transition from first-generation to second-generation believers and beyond may be usefully illuminated by two of Kierkegaard's concepts, his insistence on the offensiveness of the paradox of Christ and his idea of contemporaneity.

One of the difficulties involved in placing one's faith in an individual historical figure such as Jesus, as opposed to trusting in an abstract idea or a religious concept like nirvana or reincarnation, is how the passage of time changes the manner in which followers need to respond. The historical realities that informed the faith and made specific demands of the first generation of Jesus' disciples differed significantly from the realities of later generations, and as such the demands of faith will shift as well. On the one hand, the dynamics of faith do not change with time: every individual, no matter the generation, must still make *the leap*. And every individual's faith, regardless of the passing of the centuries, must still overcome Jesus' *offensiveness* through the same exercise of *passion* in the midst of *uncertainty*. All believers must take that 70,000-fathom plunge, but for some it is a swim through the Atlantic Ocean, whereas for others it becomes the Pacific. The realities of context affect the leap of faith; even the experience of faith's offense and uncertainty are altered by time.

Three different but related types of "shifts" occurred with the passage of time that change the nature of the offense found in Jesus. First, there was the generational shift from eyewitnesses to secondhand hearers; second, there was the cultural and religious shift from a Jewish to a Gentile audience; and finally, there was a content shift from a message about the Messiah no one expected to the proclamation of Jesus as God incarnate, Lord and Savior of the world.

Jesus' immediate contemporaries had front-row seats on his life. They could experience the gravity and/or the offensiveness of his words, acts, and demeanor for themselves as eyewitnesses. They could hear the tone of his voice, measure the expression on his face, and discuss whether the latest "miracle" had been clever sleight-of-hand or was truly inexplicable. Furthermore, the initial generation of followers was composed entirely of Jews, men and women who shared the same religious foundation and edifice as Jesus himself. Any consternation over Jesus' possible identity was defined by a shared set of general convictions about God's promises to Israel, their hope for an end-time restoration, and the possible role of a Messiah in executing God's plan. The leap required for the eyewitness generation to trust in Jesus as the Messiah no one expected was a uniquely Jewish challenge and one that came fully into focus only after the crucifixion.

But with the passing of time not only was there a gradual loss of eyewitnesses, there was also an increasing shift in the ethnicity and religious background of prospective believers. Fewer and fewer were Jews. Paul laments over Israel's hardening against the gospel even while rejoicing at the simultaneous softening of Gentile hearts instead (2 Cor. 3:7–4:6; Romans

9–11). But this means that the original obstacle to Jewish listeners — receiving Jesus as the Messiah no one expected — became less significant for Jesus' followers over time. The growing Gentile audience had no preconceived messianic hopes to measure Jesus against. They could never have experienced the gap between expectations and fulfillment (or lack thereof) that Jesus had forced open before the average Jewish listener. Perhaps the God-fearers, Gentile adherents to the synagogue, who responded to Paul's preaching in the Diaspora synagogues — the synagogues outside Israel — were exceptions to the rule. But whatever their role in the transitional stage of a church that was evolving from predominantly Jewish to Gentile assemblies, it was short-lived. The issues confronting would-be disciples changed, and the nature of the offense changed with it. There was still a chasm, but it was a chasm of a different nature. For Jewish believers in Jesus, the issue that caused offense was: How could a crucified carpenter be Israel's Messiah? For Gentile believers the question was: How could a crucified Israelite be God incarnate, Lord and Savior of the world?

It is important to nuance Kierkegaard's formulation of the offensiveness of Christian faith. In his mind, the offense rising up to combat any possibility of faith, the apparent absurdity that ties reason into knots, the paradox that can only be grasped by a leap remains the same for every generation from first to last. It is the incarnation, Jesus' claim to be the God-man, that causes the offense. Kierkegaard was a theologian who studied and trained for a pastorate in the Danish Lutheran church, and he clearly displays his orthodox *bona fides* when he makes Jesus himself the original advocate of Chalcedonian Christology:[1]

> *Directly* there was nothing to be seen [in Jesus] except a lowly human being who by signs and wonders and by claiming to be God continually constituted the possibility of offense. . . . [This lesson] is something everyone in every generation till the end of time must

---

1. *Practice in Christianity* (Princeton: Princeton University Press, 1991) 65-66. Similar passages could be multiplied many times over throughout the body of Kierkegaard's writings; for a helpful discussion of the multiple aspects of the incarnation's offensiveness in Kierkegaard's thinking, see S. Walsh, *Kierkegaard: Thinking Christianly in an Existential Mode* (Oxford: Oxford University Press, 2009) 127-31. Chalcedon was the early church council that articulated a view of Christ that persists until this day. It argued that in his humanity and divinity are exemplified two *natures* and that the one *hypostasis* of the Logos (one person) perfectly subsists in these two natures.

learn for himself from the beginning, beginning at exactly the same point as every contemporary with Christ and practicing it in the situation of contemporaneity.

For Kierkegaard, the fundamental offensiveness of the gospel for Peter, Mary, James, and Martha was no different than it is for twenty-first-century postmodernists and every generation in between. The offense appears, as the apostle Paul explains in Philippians 2:6-7, in this: "Christ Jesus . . . , being in very nature God, did not consider equality with God something to be grasped, but made himself nothing, taking the very nature of a servant, being made in human likeness" (NIV).

However, a closer and more careful reading of the Gospels makes it clear that John is the only Evangelist openly to espouse an incarnational theology. Similar formulas appear in other New Testament letters (Heb. 1:1-12; 2 Pet. 1:1), but they are most notable by their absence from the three Synoptic Gospel portraits of Jesus. It is extremely unlikely that the historical Jesus was widely vilified for frequent overt claims to be God in the flesh. In this, Kierkegaard was mistaken. Whatever seeds may have been planted in Jesus' lifetime for such ideas, an explicit incarnational theology was a decidedly post-resurrection development.

But it is not difficult to see how Jesus offended many listeners. He exercised autonomous personal authority and insisted that he was the agent of God's kingdom. Further, he generally failed to conform to any popular conceptions of messiahship. These historical clues provide a highly plausible explanation of why Jesus offended so many of his contemporaries. It is not hard to see how following Jesus during his time on earth required a passionate leap into objective uncertainty (see chapters 2 and 3 above).

In spite of the changes and regardless of the century, the culture, or the particular emphasis of the evolving proclamation, the dynamics of Christian belief remain constant. As Kierkegaard insists, no generation is allowed a direct, incremental transition to faith. There is always an unbridgeable chasm to be overcome. There is always a seeming contradiction or paradox waiting to be embraced. The conundrum that faces each person is always an occasion for offense or for faith because it always demands a headlong leap into personal, intellectual, objective uncertainty. According to Kierkegaard, everyone who passionately embraces the paradox of the gospel thereby becomes Jesus' "contemporary," no matter how many decades, centuries, or millennia separate them in time.

This nuance of Kierkegaard's view of paradox and contradiction brings us full circle to engage his perspective on what it means to truly be Jesus' contemporary, a contemporary in terms of faith rather than time. In relationship to Christ, faith overrules temporality. The passion that overcomes the offense of Jesus, however that offense is construed, creates a personal relationship between the Nazarene and the believer. This is something mere temporal or spatial proximity alone could never do. An immediate contemporary who walked away from Jesus in unbelief, someone like the rich man described in Mark 10 (see chapter 3), was not genuinely contemporary with Jesus. Such a person actually refuses to "live" in Jesus' presence, walk with him, receive his benefits, and obey his personal demands.

Modern-day believers, separated from Jesus by twenty-one centuries of meandering history, nevertheless become Jesus' genuine contemporaries by placing their faith in the resurrected One. Faith seals a personal encounter, producing the only type of contemporaneity that matters. Just as no generation is ever allowed a direct transition to Christian faith because every individual must make the leap of faith, so no one in any generation becomes a follower "at second hand" since no one ever takes that leap for another. Every individual must leap for herself. There are no secondhand followers, only the immediacy of each individual's firsthand choice.

> [T]he real contemporary is not that by virtue of immediate contemporaneity but by virtue of something else. Thus, despite his being contemporary, a contemporary can be a noncontemporary; the genuine contemporary is the genuine contemporary not by virtue of immediate contemporaneity; *ergo* the noncontemporary (in the sense of immediacy) must be able to be a contemporary by way of the something else by which a contemporary becomes a genuine contemporary . . . consequently, someone who comes later must be able to be the genuine contemporary.[2]

That "something else" which establishes true contemporaneity is the passion of faith. Having taken the necessary leap into uncertainty by believing, the real contemporary now stands with Jesus on his side of the historical, religious, personal divide. The believer that is a contemporary is

2. *Philosophical Fragments* (Princeton: Princeton University Press, 1985) 67.

now related by obedience to the historical Jesus. It does not matter that the object of faith is twenty-one centuries older than the follower. Embracing the paradox of Christ and becoming a contemporary go hand in hand, for the "eyes of faith" may only be one's own,[3] just as the leap is only taken by the individual who sees the need.

> In relation to the absolute, there is only one time, the present; for the person who is not contemporary with the absolute, it does not exist at all. And since Christ is the absolute it is easy to see that in relation to him there is only one situation, the situation of contemporaneity; the three, the seven . . . the eighteen hundred years make no difference at all; they do not change him, but neither do they reveal who he was, for who he is revealed only to faith. . . . The past is not actuality — for me. Only the contemporary is actuality for me. That with which you are living simultaneously is actuality — for you. Thus every human being is able to become contemporary only with the time in which he is living — and then with one more, with Christ's life upon earth.[4]

Such contemporaneity makes the believing individual obediently available to Christ. Knowledge and research alone can never accomplish this. I may investigate the minutiae of peasant life in first-century Palestine, learn Aramaic, and memorize ancient texts, but none of this will make me Jesus' contemporary. But if I make myself obediently available to the presence of Christ in my life, that *will* make me his contemporary.

This is in effect what Paul intends when he calls unbelievers to "the obedience of faith." The apostle tells the church at Rome, "Through [Christ Jesus] and for his name's sake, we received grace and apostleship to call people from among all the Gentiles to *the obedience of faith* (or the obedience *which is* faith). *And you also are among those who are called to belong to Jesus Christ*" (Rom. 1:5-6 NIV).[5] By responding in faith to the gos-

---

3. Kierkegaard defines faith as "autopsy" — seeing with one's own eyes; *Philosophical Fragments,* 70, 102.

4. *Practice in Christianity,* 63-64.

5. See the discussion of faith as obedience in R. Bultmann, *Theology of the New Testament* (New York: Scribner, 1951) 314-19. Bultmann is reflecting the pervasive influence of Kierkegaard (whether or not it is mediated by Heidegger) on his thinking about the contrast between the gospel (which requires action) and theology (which is content with thought

pel, the Roman believers have leaped obediently to stand alongside the resurrected Jesus, belonging now to the One who called them to his side.

From Contemporary to Contemporaneity

In his watershed study *Paul and Palestinian Judaism*, E. P. Sanders observed that "The related questions of the starting point for seeing Paul's religious thought accurately and of the centre of his thinking are among the most difficult in Pauline studies."[6] It is my intent not to enter into the debate but simply to explain my starting point. Understanding Paul's life, ministry, and theological development as an apostle must begin with his encounter with the glorified Jesus on the road to Damascus.[7] Martin Hengel and A. M. Schwemer hit the nail on the head when they write, "At the beginning stands a personal encounter, a being overwhelmed by the crucified and exalted Christ."[8] Although Paul's encounter was unique insofar as it was his call to apostleship, it was also exemplary in that it was his conversion from an old to a new life, a new religious existence.[9] The long-

---

alone) when he writes: Theology must "avoid conceiving [itself] as an objectifying kind of thought cut loose from the act of living. . . . [W]hen revelation is conceived as an arrangement for the impartation of teachings, these teachings have the character of the objectifying thought of science, a kind of thought which dims their existential reference to living into a mere object of thought — but then they are pseudo-scientific teachings. . . . [The gospel] does not offer itself to critical thought but speaks into one's concrete existence. . . . [T]he statements of the kerygma are not universal truths but are personal address in a concrete situation" (2:240-41).

6. *Paul and Palestinian Judaism: A Comparison of Patterns of Religion* (Philadelphia: Fortress, 1977) 433.

7. The work of Seyoon Kim, *The Origin of Paul's Gospel* (Tübingen: Mohr, 1981) remains essential on this point. Also see the important though often neglected work of J. G. Machen, *The Origin of Paul's Religion* (New York: Macmillan, 1921) 56-68; also M. E. Thrall, "The Origin of Pauline Christology," in *Apostolic History and the Gospel* (ed. W. W. Gasque and R. P. Martin; Grand Rapids: Eerdmans, 1970) 304-16; C. Dietzfelbinger, *Die Berufung des Paulus als Ursprung seiner Theologie* (Neukirchen-Vluyn: Neukirchener, 1985); M. Hengel and A. M. Schwemer, *Paul between Damascus and Antioch: The Unknown Years* (Louisville: Westminster John Knox, 1997) 98-105; R. N. Longenecker, ed., *The Road from Damascus: The Impact of Paul's Conversion on His Life, Thought, and Ministry* (Grand Rapids: Eerdmans, 1997).

8. *Paul between Damascus and Antioch*, 98.

9. If changing from a zealous and rigorous Pharisee into the apostle of the resurrected

standing debate over whether we should interpret Paul's experience as a conversion or as a commission is a bit like debating whether middle-aged men drive Corvettes as a means of transportation or as a status symbol (personally, I ride a Harley-Davidson). Paul certainly interpreted his encounter with Jesus as the moment of his conversion, which came with a new calling, and as such he viewed it as paradigmatic for every other believer, whether Jew or Gentile.[10] As he urges the church in Galatia, "I plead with you, brothers, become like me!" (Gal. 4:12 NIV). He understood his encounter with Christ, his conversion experience, as typical, in some way, for every believer's conversion.

So it is no surprise that Paul appeals to his readers' own conversion experiences. He assumes that their initial encounter with Christ served a formative role in their spiritual development similar to his. He freely employs an experiential, pastoral apologetic that gambles everything on his readers' ongoing belief in the truth of that startling invasion of Christ's presence into their lives when they first believed the gospel. This apostolic strategy obviously involved serious risk. To have such an appeal acting as the foundation of Paul's argument means that his apologetic is not built on logic but is thoroughly subjective and experiential.[11] Though Paul builds a rational argument from his appeal to experience — if you have experienced this, then x, y, and z must be the case — logical argument per se is not the cornerstone. The extraordinary nature of that initial experience will always provide a seemingly weak flank open to the wolves of skeptical, rational at-

---

Christ who sets aside the need for Torah observance, including the necessity of circumcision for community membership, is not the replacement of one religious pattern for another, then I don't know what would qualify; also see Bultmann, *Theology of the New Testament,* 1:188-89. A. Segal, *Paul the Convert: The Apostolate and Apostasy of Saul the Pharisee* (New Haven: Yale University Press, 1990) 128 notes, "When he was a Pharisee, Paul would have been incapable of saying that faith rather than law manifests the righteousness of God in any meaningful way. No other Jews in the first century distinguish faith and law in the way Paul does."

10. Segal makes this point very thoroughly in *Paul the Convert;* also see R. Bultmann, "Paul," in *Existence and Faith: Shorter Writings of Rudolf Bultmann* (New York: Meridian, 1970) 122. The point was stated clearly by J. E. Rattenbury, *The Religious Experience of St. Paul* (Nashville: Cokesbury, 1931) 60: "The great value of Paul's knowledge of Jesus is that it is the only sort of knowledge we can have of Jesus today — the only sort of direct knowledge."

11. R. Hays provides a good analysis of how Paul similarly risks making spiritual experience the foundation of his biblical hermeneutics; see *Echoes of Scripture in the Letters of Paul* (New Haven: Yale University Press, 1989) 107-11.

tack.[12] The danger is that eventually some members of Paul's churches might yield to the kinds of intellectual or psychological pressures that can eventually snuff out a young enthusiast's spiritual flame. If a Pauline believer comes to reject the reality of his or her once-precious conversion story, then Paul has lost the common ground that makes his pastoral appeals possible. Conversation comes to a halt. But this did not intimidate Paul or prevent him from teaching theology as the flowering plant that blooms from the fertile soil of the common experience with Christ.

Paul Makes the Leap

The obvious place to begin investigating Paul's experience is his letter to the Galatians. Here Paul describes a surprising about-face from his previous life as a confident, zealous, Pharisaic persecutor of the early church (Gal. 1:13-14). He appeals to the revelation of God's Son made to him (or "in him," v. 16a) on the Damascus road (vv. 15-16; cf. Acts 9:1-18; 22:3-21; 26:4-18). He emphatically insists that no human instruction was involved in this turn-around. His claim is that he received the gospel of Jesus Christ, in its basic form, directly from Jesus. Furthermore, the outworking of its many religious implications occurred in personal conversation between Paul and the Lord alone (Gal. 1:11-12, 16-24).[13]

The views of Krister Stendahl, E. P. Sanders and other representatives of what is sometimes called the "new perspective" on Paul are now widely accepted. Still, in concert with such interpreters, it is worth repeating here

12. In this regard, I. W. Scott usefully analyzes Paul's epistemology as coherentist, necessarily including non-rational factors, rather than foundationalist; see *Paul's Way of Knowing: Story, Experience, and the Spirit* (Grand Rapids: Baker, 2006) 280-87.

13. This is my principal critique of Segal's otherwise illuminating study. Having begun by insisting that Paul's autobiographical accounts of his conversion are more historically reliable than the biographical narratives in the book of Acts, Segal then repeatedly ignores Paul's own insistence that his gospel was not formulated in consultation with anyone but the Lord himself. Thus, Segal's thesis that Paul's gospel was largely shaped by his early (pre-conversion) association with Gentile Christianity is oddly contrary to his stated method. Furthermore, Segal never explains by what stretch of the imagination we are to believe that Saul, the Pharisee from Tarsus, would submit his numerous mystical experiences of heavenly "glory" (assuming that Saul practiced a form of merkabah mysticism) to be interpreted for him as the manifestation of the resurrected Jesus by a largely uncircumcised Gentile Christian community; see *Paul the Convert*, 29-30, 37-38, 58, 66, 69-71, 75, 113, 117, and passim.

that there is virtually no evidence that Paul came to faith in Christ through the prodding of an overworked conscience or by any sense of inadequacy in his Judaism.[14] Quite the opposite. Paul's autobiographical snippets testify to a clear, stainless, healthy conscience possessed by a bold, zealous, and pious Pharisee who was perfectly content in his lifelong faith as a child of Abraham (Gal. 1:11-14; Phil. 3:4b-6).[15] Pauline Christianity did not arise as a remedy to some previously imperceptible failing in pre-Christian Judaism;[16] at least, that was not Paul's view of his apostleship. This important conclusion is the foundation underlying Sanders's famous summary statement that, for this apostle, "the solution [i.e., faith in Christ] precedes the problem [i.e., the absence of God's righteousness]," not the other way around.[17] In other words, Paul was not a guilty man subconsciously in search of a savior. He was, in fact, a religiously satisfied man searching for ways to eradicate permanently the memory of a messianic pretender from the hearts and minds of his Jewish followers.

Even though Paul may not have shared in the West's "introspective conscience," as Stendahl has warned us to remember,[18] any pious Pharisee like Saul would certainly have possessed a robust facility at conscientious

14. See the discussion of Romans 7 below in this chapter. For a representative sample of the continuing scholarly debate over the new perspective, see Sanders, *Paul and Palestinian Judaism;* D. A. Carson et al., eds., *Justification and Variegated Nomism: A Fresh Appraisal of Paul and Second Temple Judaism* (2 vols.; Tübingen: Mohr, 2001); S. Kim, *Paul and the New Perspective: Second Thoughts on the Origin of Paul's Gospel* (Grand Rapids: Eerdmans, 2002); F. Watson, *Paul, Judaism, and the Gentiles: Beyond the New Perspective* (rev. ed.; Grand Rapids: Eerdmans, 2007); J. D. G. Dunn, *The New Perspective on Paul* (rev. ed.; Grand Rapids: Eerdmans, 2008).

15. In commenting on Gal. 1:14, Dunn, *New Perspective*, 359 observes, "[I]n these words we hear the authentic voice of [a] late Second Temple Pharisee, as Paul recalls his pre-conversion understanding of what it meant to live 'in Judaism.'"

16. I am painfully aware of the anachronism of this otherwise usefully descriptive label.

17. *Paul and Palestinian Judaism*, 442-44, 474-76, 481-84, 490, 495-501, 506-7, 510, 554-55.

18. K. Stendahl, "The Apostle Paul and the Introspective Conscience of the West," *Harvard Theological Review* 56 (1963): 115-215, reprinted in *Paul among Jews and Gentiles* (Philadelphia: Fortress, 1976) 78-96; for a critique of Stendahl, see B. Corley, "Interpreting Paul's Conversion — Then and Now," in Longenecker, ed., *The Road from Damascus*, 1-17. Stendahl's position was anticipated by W. Wrede; in fact, by attempting to refute Wrede's arguments, both P. Gardner and J. E. Rattenbury provide an early example of the continuing debate over Paul's guilty conscience; see Gardner, *The Religious Experience of Saint Paul* (New York: Putnam, 1911) 25-33; Rattenbury, *The Religious Experience of St. Paul: Studies in Doctrines Born of Evangelical Experience* (Nashville: Cokesbury, 1931) 14-16.

introspection. Paul's letters do provide significant evidence of this sort of self-evaluation after his dramatic encounter with Christ. In fact, after an experience such as the one described on the road to Damascus, it is difficult not to imagine Paul frantically asking himself, "How could I have been so wrong?" It would have been inevitable; he would have finely sifted through all the details of his lifelong belief system searching for the fatal flaw.

As Paul attempted to regather himself from this startling heavenly assault on his sense of personal identity and life purpose, he would have questioned himself. He would have asked how all of his previous religious devotion — true devotion offered to the one, true God — had not only failed to prepare him for the Messiah when he came, but had actually blinded him of all people, a devout Pharisee, to the Messiah's identity in Jesus.[19]

The pre-conversion Saul may not have been plagued by a guilty conscience, but the post-conversion Paul exercised a very harsh retrospective evaluation of this prior piety. Paul concludes that "whatever was to my benefit I now consider to have been loss. In fact, I now think of those things as wasted" (Phil. 3:8). All of Paul's former zeal in the ways of his ancestors is described *retrospectively* as spiritual refuse, rubbish that was actually detrimental to apprehending the message of Jesus. Again, Paul never suggests that the detriment was somehow intrinsic to his Pharisaism. He never claims that it arose through a guilt complex or that he ever harbored such reservations prior to his conversion. There simply was no process of personal reflection that led Paul to evolve from Pharisaism to Christian discipleship. He was no apostolic butterfly grown from a Pharisaic caterpillar. Had Paul attempted to make such arguments, he would have been constructing a direct connection (to use Kierkegaard's terms) from his previous to his subsequent spiritual life, *something he never does*.[20] An im-

---

19. Though Sanders argues that Paul focuses not on Jesus' role as Messiah but on the fact that "Jesus Christ is Lord," observing that Paul's conversion involves recognizing Jesus' messiahship is not to claim that messiahship is the starting point for Paul's theology; see *Paul and Palestinian Judaism*, 514-15. Certainly, the proclamation of "Jesus *Christ* as Lord" is evidence that Paul confessed Jesus' messiahship, something Saul would never have done, whether his Hellenistic audiences understood *Christos* as a title or as a proper name.

20. The same may be said of those who still insist on a pre-conversion guilty conscience as the key to Paul's transformation. This position not only runs counter to the evidence but also offers an academic attempt to build another reasonable, quantitative bridge directly from unbelief to belief.

mediate transition, to use Kierkegaard's phrase once again, from Pharisee to apostle simply did not exist for Paul any more than it existed for the original circle of the Twelve (or for any believer today). Naturally, Paul need not confirm Kierkegaard's understanding of faith, but it is worth noting how closely Kierkegaard's analysis of faith conforms to Paul's own psychological description of his conversion experience. Unlike the butterfly, this apostle's rebirth was more like Athena, the goddess of wisdom. In Greek mythology, she sprung fully formed from Zeus's forehead. So Paul's gospel was not a product of evolution but was created whole cloth from the risen Jesus.

Paul is reading his life in reverse, not constructing a bridge from old to new or a line of direct transition from his pre- to his post-conversion sensibilities. The only thing linking Saul the Pharisee to Paul the Apostle is the uninvited, intrusive, heavenly revelation of the exalted Jesus on the Damascus road. In Paul's own description, there are no promise-fulfillment, type-antitype, or shadow-reality notions anywhere in sight. Paul never seeks to construct such reasonable explanations of his transformation. He never points to anything at all from his religious past as having been the least bit preparatory or "sensitizing" for his eventual discovery of "fulfillment" in Jesus.

Paul explicitly emphasizes the reevaluative power of his spiritual awakening in a crucial passage that places the recognition of Jesus' identity at center-stage. Paul writes: "From now on I don't evaluate anyone from a human vantage point; although I did once evaluate Christ from a human perspective, I don't any longer" (2 Cor. 5:16). Paul never asserted that he had stumbled over his Judaism or Torah observance. Rather, *he had been offended by the historical Jesus,* or at least by the nascent church's proclamation about Jesus. Regarding the Galilean preacher "from a human point of view" had entailed measuring him against the current national religious expectations of what a possible Messiah might look like.[21] We have already seen that the crucified, resurrected Jesus did not fit into any preexisting notions of what the Messiah should be (chapter 2). Further, we have no idea what Paul's pre-conversion, messianic expectations may have been, if he had any at all. But that is not his point in 2 Corinthians 5:16. He gives a

---

21. Kim, *Origin,* 14-15, 18, 107-8, 312; cf. Bultmann, *Theology,* 1:294: "Any 'evaluation' of the historical person Jesus according to human categories would be *kata sarka* [from a human point of view]."

pivotal role in his thought to Deuteronomy 21:23: "anyone who is hung on a tree is under God's curse" (NIV). Further, in Galatians 3:10-14 he describes the crucifixion as a curse. Thus, for Paul, it appears more likely that the accursed Messiah proclaimed by the church as Son of God would have been a blasphemous oxymoron fueling his vehement hostility.[22] Paul is no doubt reflecting his own antagonism to the preaching of the early church in 1 Corinthians 1:23 when he explains that the gospel of a crucified Christ was "to Jews a scandal or cause of offense."[23] That message would have been as shocking for Paul as telling an American Fundamentalist that the Son of Man would return at the head of a gay-pride parade.

When confronted with the Messiah no one expected, a crucified carpenter condemned by the law, Paul had quite understandably embraced offense rather than faith. Paul's eventual rejection of Torah as the way to righteousness was most probably informed first and foremost by this staggering incongruity: a man condemned as accursed by Torah was in fact the Messiah, who had been resurrected and exalted by God! How could God's own law have proved so misleading?

When Paul reminds the Galatians that "Christ became a curse on our behalf, because it is written, 'Cursed is everyone who is hanged on a tree'" (Gal. 3:13, citing Deut. 21:23) he may well be recalling his own past appeal to Deuteronomy 21:23 as the Torah-based justification for his rejection of the ludicrous proposition that Jesus of Nazareth was God's Messiah.[24] However, after the Damascus experience, the newly minted apostle — clean conscience and healthy devotion intact — began the process of embracing an unexpectedly new perspective. The advent of a resurrected, vindicated Jesus recast, or even possibly abrogated, the place of Torah in assuring righteousness before God. Through no fault of his own, keeping his eyes focused on

---

22. Kim, *Origin*, 46-49, 105, 126, 270, 274-75, 280-81; A. J. Hultgren, "Paul's Pre-Christian Persecutions of the Church: Their Purpose, Locale, and Nature," *Journal of Biblical Literature* 95 (1976): 102-4, 110; F. F. Bruce, *Paul, Apostle of the Heart Set Free* (Grand Rapids: Eerdmans, 1977) 70-71; M. Hengel, *Crucifixion in the Ancient World and the Folly of the Message of the Cross* (Philadelphia: Fortress, 1977) 2-4, 84-87; *The Atonement: The Origins of the Doctrine in the New Testament* (Philadelphia: Fortress, 1981) 43-44; Dietzfelbinger, *Berufung*, 36-42. This conclusion is not intended to exclude other supplementary motives such as offense at the inclusion of uncircumcised Gentiles within the covenant community.

23. Dunn, *New Perspective*, 350-51.

24. As Dunn notes, Qumran has confirmed that this Deuteronomic curse had been applied to the act of crucifixion by the time of Jesus and Paul (see 4QpNah 1:7-8; 11QT 64:6-13; *New Perspective*, 35).

Torah had blinded Paul to the real Jesus. It was in the end a fresh vision of Jesus that recast Paul's perception of Torah.

Paul Appeals to Others

Having received his apostolic commission, Paul often mentions the profound sense of obligation compelling him to proclaim the message of Jesus Christ as the resurrected and ascended Lord (Rom. 1:1; 15:16; 1 Cor. 4:1-2; 9:16; 2 Cor. 5:14; Col. 1:25; 1 Thess. 2:4). Crucial to Paul's sense of urgency was his belief that the gospel, when proclaimed faithfully, creates new spiritual opportunities similar to his experience on the Damascus road. The gospel was more than a message to be heard and then acknowledged or discounted. The proclamation of this message went beyond mere verbal communication. Proclaiming the good news actually called forth the saving presence of the resurrected Lord, just as rubbing one's hand against the burnished side of a long lost Arabian lamp calls forth a powerful genie. Preaching the gospel was an act of *re-presenting* the resurrected, living Jesus to listeners. In witnessing that moment of proclamation, becoming contemporary with Jesus through faith is a renewed possibility, over and over again.

Recalling his early days of preaching to the not yet converted Galatians, Paul is absolutely emphatic: "*Before your very eyes* Jesus Christ was *clearly portrayed* as crucified" (Gal. 3:1 NIV). Paul is convinced that preaching is reality-depicting just as believing is truly seeing. More than that, explaining the good news effects a new reality, the spiritual presence of Christ with the listener. Paul did not work as the master of ceremonies at some ancient puppet show with stick figurines dramatizing an early version of the Passion Play. He proclaimed the gospel. He trusted the Spirit to enflame his listeners' imaginations. With such empowerment, the images "clearly portrayed" before their "very eyes" were more like a fresh incarnation. The spiritual realities were being molded, pressed, and finally given birth through the apostle's words, offered there and then in the *real presence* of the resurrected Jesus to each and every hearer.

In this way, the Galatian believers became "eyewitnesses" to Christ's crucifixion and exaltation. In hearing and receiving the gospel they were made contemporaries of Jesus as they encountered him for themselves. Paul knew this to be true because they professed their faith in the resurrection and made themselves obediently available to Christ's service. And just as Paul recalled his own response to the Damascus vision, so he took the Galatians back to the supernatural experiences once initiated by their leap of faith: "Does[n't] God give you his Spirit and work miracles among you . . . because you believe what you heard?" (Gal. 3:5 NIV; cf. 1 Thess. 1:5; 2:13; 2 Thess. 2:14). Again, Paul makes an experiential appeal to a new spiritual quality of existence initiated by faith in the gospel.

Similarly, as Paul concludes his letter to the Romans, he explains how such supernatural experiences serve as his letters of confirmation to a church he has never visited: "I will not venture to speak of anything except what Christ has accomplished through me in leading the Gentiles to obey God by what I have said and done — *by the power of signs and miracles, through the power of the Spirit*" (Rom. 15:18-19 NIV). Such confirmatory happenings need not be extraordinary or supra-rational. They may also consist in the awakening of Christian community and personal, ethical transformation as in the church at Philippi: "If you have any encouragement from being united with Christ, if any comfort from his love, if any fellowship with the Spirit, if any tenderness and compassion, then make my joy complete by being like-minded, having the same love, being one in spirit and purpose" (Phil. 2:1-2). What if the Philippians had responded, "No. We have never experienced any of these things — no encouragement, no unity with Christ, nothing like that"? Paul's pastoral appeal would have remained utterly toothless. But he does not hesitate to presume upon such shared experiences. He subjects such moments to a common Christological explanation. In believing Paul's gospel, every believer has a personal encounter with Jesus Christ, becoming his immediate contemporary, subject to his personal influence.

Paul dovetails his response to Christ with his listeners' conversion to the gospel most thoroughly in 2 Corinthians 3:7–4:6. A broad, scholarly consensus maintains that Paul is here contrasting Jesus' appearance to him on the Damascus road with Yahweh's Mount Sinai appearance to Moses in Exodus 33:18–34:7 (see especially 2 Cor. 3:7-18 and 4:3-5).[25] At the same time, Paul is also describing his conversion as exemplary for every other

25. See Kim, *Origin*, 5-13, 229-39; Segal, *Paul the Convert*, 60-61; M. E. Thrall, *A Critical and Exegetical Commentary on the Second Epistle to the Corinthians* (Edinburgh: Clark, 1994) 1:315-20; J. D. G. Dunn, *The Theology of the Apostle Paul* (Grand Rapids: Eerdmans, 1998) 290; M. J. Harris, *The Second Epistle to the Corinthians: A Commentary on the Greek Text* (Grand Rapids: Eerdmans, 2005) 336-37.

believer (especially in 2 Cor. 3:18; 4:6). As such, Paul both makes himself the antitype to Moses[26] and the prototype for every Christian. The glory of Yahweh once revealed to Moses at Mount Sinai is now forever expressed in the glory of Christ (Acts 9:3; 22:6, 11; 26:13). The divine *shekinah,* the Hebrew word that refers to the Lord's glorious *indwelling,* is now shining on everyone who believes the good news. The Lord is the Spirit and as the Spirit impresses an individual with the truth of the gospel. Christ reveals himself in glory: "And we, who with unveiled faces all reflect the Lord's glory are being transformed into his likeness with ever-increasing glory, which comes from the Lord, who is the Spirit" (2 Cor. 3:18); "for God, who said, 'Let light shine out of darkness,' made his light shine in our hearts to give us the light of the knowledge of the glory of God in the face of Christ" (4:6). But this does not just parallel Moses and Paul's visions of God's glory. There are also significant contrasts between the divine appearance made at Sinai and the revelation on the road to Damascus. For Moses, the glory faded, but the glory shown to Paul continues in his ministry.

These two aspects of similarity and dissimilarity working together make possible the exemplary role of Paul's experience for every other believer. Paul's own dramatic transformation from Pharisee to apostle with his reevaluation of his own participation in the Sinai covenant serves as a template. His experience and reflection undergird his unwavering conviction that future christophanies, revelations of Jesus generated by the Holy Spirit, will be given to anyone coming to faith. Anyone who willingly overcomes the offense of the gospel through faith will share the life of Jesus now. The "fading glory" of the old covenant has given way once and for all, like a flickering candle suddenly overwhelmed by a bright spotlight. The old covenant is now engulfed by the "surpassing glory" of new life in the Spirit and of the ministry that brings true righteousness (2 Cor. 3:7-18).

"Whenever anyone turns to the Lord, the veil is taken away" (2 Cor. 3:16 NIV). Paul is alluding here to the story of Moses who, having seen the glory of God, returned to the people of Israel and covered his transfigured face with a veil because the people were afraid to look at him (Exod. 34:30).

26. "Of Paul's many new and startling utterances, this is perhaps the most surprising. The greatest man in the history of Israel is put beneath the traveling tent-maker." J. Munck, *Paul and the Salvation of Mankind* (Atlanta: John Knox, 1959) 61; also R. P. Martin, *2 Corinthians* (Waco: Word, 1986) 67; C. K. Stockhausen, *Moses' Veil and the Glory of the New Covenant: The Exegetical Substructure of II Cor. 3,1–4,6* (Rome: Pontifical Biblical Institute, 1989) 169-75.

But Paul also remembers that Moses did not wear the veil constantly; he removed it each time he returned to Yahweh's presence (Exod. 34:34). In God's presence, Moses' unveiled face reflected the Lord's glory, and he replaced the veil when he left God's presence. Paul makes subtle use of this pattern to make his own point about the power of the gospel: wearing the veil symbolizes standing outside God's presence, and everyone who rejects the gospel is separated from God, but every believer becomes a new Moses when she sees Christ.[27] Accepting Jesus Christ as Lord demonstrates that the old veil, now representing spiritual blindness, has been lifted. Believers now reside in the presence of Yahweh's *shekinah* glory, gazing into the face of Jesus Christ just as Moses unveiled once communed with God (2 Cor. 3:18; 4:5). So, just as Paul is paralleled with Moses, the Christian is paralleled with both Moses and Paul. Believing the gospel makes one contemporary with Christ, which is like seeing the heavenly Jesus revealed on the Damascus road, which is like seeing the glory of Yahweh on Mount Sinai.

Paul's repeated emphasis on immediate contemporaneity should not be overlooked in these comparisons. In his mind, Scripture insists that Moses actually "saw" as much of Yahweh's presence as was humanly tolerable. Moses was in God's immediate presence. Paul also actually "saw," whether through internal illumination or by external presence, and conversed with the heavenly Jesus. Now he further insists that when anyone hears the gospel, they share in the living presence of the exalted Jesus. The gospel is not simply information about Jesus but the actual person of Jesus offering himself to everyone who listens. When faith refuses to be waylaid by the apparent absurdity of that statement, contemporaneity with Christ is created. This contemporaneity is every bit as genuine for the Christian as it was for Moses and Paul.

Rereading Scripture with an Apostolic Imagination

In chapter 2 we examined the thoroughgoing way in which the New Testament writers, including Paul, reinterpret the Old Testament according to

27. So J. Héring, *The Second Epistle of Saint Paul to the Corinthians* (London: Epworth, 1967) 27, n. 21. Segal suggests that Paul also has in mind the Jewish use of prayer shawls or *tallit* to cover the heads of men during individual and communal prayer or Torah reading (*Paul the Convert*, 152-54). If this is the case, then Paul's critique of his Judaizing opponents and their worship practices becomes all the sharper.

the creative dictates of a new, gospel-inspired imagination. Here we need only to look briefly at the way Paul dovetails such reinterpretation in Galatians 3:13; 2 Corinthians 3:14-16; and Romans 7:7-24 with elements of his own conversion experience. What becomes apparent is an existential lens through which Paul reads both Scripture and his own past. This in turn buttresses the way he relates his personal experience to his apostolic teaching.

Galatians 3:13

Earlier I suggested that Saul's hostility to the early church was, at least in part, fueled by his understanding of Deuteronomy 21:23, ". . . anyone who is hung on a tree is under God's curse" (NIV). Because of this passage, a crucified Messiah would have seemed an impossible oxymoron to any thoughtful Jew. However, after seeing and hearing the exalted Jesus, the crucified Messiah vindicated rather than cursed by God, Paul was forced to reconsider the role of Torah in God's new economy.[28] Two parallel trajectories seem to follow in his mind.

First, the resurrection, and thus the vindication, of God's Messiah had flatly contradicted the law and shown it to be wrong. The crucified One was most decidedly *not* cursed by God. In fact, God's actions had subverted his own word. Thus, Paul's Damascus encounter demonstrated that a right relationship with God is discovered through faith in the glorified Jesus, not through adherence to the now contravened Torah.

Second, Jesus was cursed on the cross but the curse was not from God, as Deuteronomy 21:23 had warned. Deuteronomy mentions another curse in 27:26: "Cursed is the man who does not uphold the words of this law by carrying them out" (NIV). Paul cites this legal text in Galatians 3:10, demonstrating how closely the two curse passages had come to be linked in his mind. Clearly, Jesus had not been cursed by God, but the two Deuteronomy curse passages remain relevant in conjunction with each other. The law's abrogation is linked to the human failure to keep it perfectly (Gal. 3:10). This had not been Paul's past experience with Torah, but in the light of his Damascus encounter, he had been driven to this new conclusion.

---

28. See Kim, *Origin*, 274-75; Hengel and Schwemer, *Paul between Damascus and Antioch*, 98-101, 103-5.

Consequently, Jesus had borne the curse *of the law* rather than the curse of God, and this on our behalf. Jesus thereby becomes our substitute: "Christ redeemed us from the curse of the law, becoming a curse on our behalf" (Gal. 3:13).

God had contravened his own law, the law became a curse for us, and therefore the Messiah was crucified for any who believe in him. This line of reasoning would never have occurred to Saul the Pharisee. Nothing we know about Jewish methods of biblical interpretation would have compelled Saul to such unexpected "insights." But in speaking from heaven and knocking the spiritual stuffing out of a zealous Pharisee, the exalted Jesus demanded that Paul begin to utterly reimagine his old way of reading, thinking, and believing.

2 Corinthians 3:14-16

We have already seen the creative use Paul makes of Moses' veil, transforming it into a symbol of Israel's spiritual obduracy in rejecting Jesus. One may have expected Paul to take this as an occasion for elaborating on Israel's misbehavior. Or he might have developed his discussion of Moses' broader ministry to the nation. Or Paul might have demonstrated how a right reading of the books of Moses would point the reader to Christ. But he does no such thing. Instead, he explicitly says three times in quick succession that such Christian understanding is the very thing Scripture reading alone cannot produce. Scripture is now grasped correctly only after the individual encounters Christ and believes:

> Their minds were hardened. For to this very day, the same veil remains when the old covenant is read; it has not been removed, because only in Christ is it taken away. (v. 14b)

> But even to this day, whenever Moses is read, a veil lies over their heart. (v. 15)

> But whenever anyone turns to the Lord, the veil is removed. (v. 16)

According to Paul, Scripture study alone, no matter how fervently a student works at it, can never build a bridge to faith in Jesus. The process must work the other way around, from faith to understanding. Only in the exercise of faith, that is, by embracing the paradox of a crucified Messiah who subverts God's law, is unanticipated by the Scriptures, and turns God's law into a curse, will any reader find the eyes needed to read Scripture correctly. In other words, 2 Corinthians 3:14-16 lays out the interpretive principle at work in such texts as Galatians 3:13. Here Paul clarifies how his faith illuminates his rereading of the Deuteronomic curses in relation to the law, crucifixion, the Messiah, and faith. Understanding happens backward in the light of faith.

Romans 7

Finally, we may briefly comment on the importance of Paul's conclusions about the law in Romans 7.[29] Though this passage is very complex and often debated, for my purposes here it suffices to say that I understand Paul's argument as a retrospective reinterpretation of his life, past and present, from a Christian point of view:[30]

1. Introductory analogy: death liberates from the law (vv. 1-3).
2. Having shared in Christ's death, the believer is freed from the law in order to "serve in the new way of the Spirit" (vv. 4-6; cf. Gal. 5:16-26).
3. Paul's experience is the same as all of humanity's since in Adam ("I") we experience the law as an instrument of sin and death, although the law itself remains holy (vv. 7-12).
4. Paul reflects on his own divided self ("I"), an existential contradiction born of the eschatological tension (the "already/not yet" split) created by Christ's advent (vv. 13-25): the power of sin and death described in vv. 7-12 continues as before, but for the believer that level of existence now coexists with the new work of the Spirit described in vv. 4-6.

29. The seminal work on this passage remains W. G. Kümmel, "Römer 7 und die Bekehrung des Paulus," in *Römer 7 und das Bild des Menschen im Neuen Testament* (Munich: Kaiser, 1974); for a history and survey of interpretation, see E. Wasserman, *The Death of the Soul in Romans 7* (Tübingen: Mohr, 2008) 1-13, 51-60; for a summary of the possible identities of the "I" in vv. 7-25, see J. Lambrecht, *The Wretched "I" and Its Liberation: Paul in Romans 7 and 8* (Grand Rapids: Eerdmans, 1992) 59-91.

30. As does Bultmann, *Theology,* 1:247. I generally agree with the exposition offered by J. D. G. Dunn, *Romans 1–8* (Dallas: Word, 1988) 357-412.

In his wildest dreams, Saul the Pharisee would never have imagined that one day he would describe the law of God, the divine gift for life and righteousness within the covenant, as an instrument of sin and death. However, this is precisely what Paul the apostle concludes. Romans 7 reveals how Paul's past convictions, including his own self-understanding, have been turned topsy-turvy by faith in Christ. Such pivotal phrases as "you died to the law" (v. 4), "we were controlled by the flesh" (v. 5), "the law aroused sinful passions" (v. 5), "we bore fruit for death" (v. 5), "we have been released from the law" (v. 6), "apart from the law sin is dead" (v. 7), and "I was alive apart from the law" (v. 9) are not drawn from Paul's memories of Pharisaism but offer a Christian reappraisal of his past Pharisaism. The Pharisee's confident boast of blamelessness with respect to the law (Phil. 3:4-6) is now corrected by the Christian perspective explained in Romans 7:7-12. Paul comes to realize that he was never really blameless at all, but it required a head-on collision with heaven to show him the error of his ways. Studying the law per se had never revealed this to him.

Similarly, the internal wrestling match that culminates in the anguished outcry of Romans 7:24, "Wretched man that I am! Who will rescue me from this body of death?" (NIV), is not evidence of a Pharisee's stricken conscience. Rather this outcry testifies to the apostle's (and every sensitive believer's) frustrated awareness that he or she is simultaneously empowered "to serve in the new way of the Spirit" (v. 6) while remaining "a prisoner to the law of sin at work within my members" (v. 23).[31] Like ev-

---

31. I confess that I find Stendahl's influential work "Introspective Conscience" dismissive and abstruse in its discussion of these verses. Stendahl argues against the view taken here by making three points: first, Romans 7 is making an argument about the law, not about anthropology; second, the confession in vv. 15 and 19 does not lead immediately to the lament of v. 24 (as one would expect of a true penitent) but to personal acquittal (vv. 16-17, 20: "If I do what I do not want to do . . . it is no longer I myself who do it"); third, Paul's "distinction between the good Law and the bad Sin is based on the rather trivial observation that every man knows that there is a difference between what he ought to do and what he does" (93). It strikes me that all three points are a type of argument *ad verecundiam* where Stendahl merely speaks as his own authority, expecting the reader to acquiesce. First, it is not hard to understand how an argument about the law might also give considerable attention to the experiences of those who are obliged to keep the law. Second, Paul is able to acquit his own ego of sin while simultaneously lamenting the fact that he does the very things he does not want to do because his ego has been crucified with Christ (vv. 4-6) and is therefore no longer able to incur guilt (vv. 17, 20) while he continues to wrestle with the power of his own "flesh" (v. 18, 25b) until the parousia (v. 25a). Third, for the individual feeling trapped by self-

eryone else, Paul is living his life forward while interpreting it backward. Paul interprets in reverse because, along with every other convert to Christ, Paul has experienced the sharp discontinuity between his past and his present. Paul faced an existential gulf overcome only by making the leap of faith after having a personal encounter with Christ.

Seeing Jesus Today

Appealing to experience as the logical foundation for a religious argument is always a ticklish business. What distinguishes legitimate from illegitimate experiences, true from false, authentic from inauthentic? Is there even such a thing as an illegitimate, false, or inauthentic experience? Isn't any experience a "true" experience for the one who experiences it, as a matter of definition? We have seen that Paul is not deterred by these issues from using experiential arguments. Although he does not go into great detail as to how we can answer the questions of distinguishing true from false experiences, we can discern some implicit guidelines that will prove helpful.

Paul views religious experience from two vantage points simultaneously, one general and the other specific. On the one hand, he speaks of spiritual experience very broadly when he appeals to the evidentiary value of the whole of the Christian life. Whether referring to overtly supernatural moments such as miracles and other acts of power (Gal. 3:5; Rom. 15:19), or to more day-to-day experiences of comfort, encouragement, and corporate fellowship (Phil. 2:1), Paul views the entirety of the Christian life as equally miraculous. Anything and everything traceable back to "life in Christ," no matter how commonplace, provides experiential testimony to Christ's presence in a believer's life. The overtly supernatural carries no greater weight, in this regard, than, say, the persistent experience of peace in a time of trial. Paul would insist that outside Christ the unbeliever is no more able to conjure the one than the other, the overtly supernatural or the persistent. Perhaps, persistently resting in God's grace through all of life's ups and downs is the greater miracle after all. We simply cannot prejudge what type of sensory, psychological, emotional, or physical alterations must accompany "valid" spiritual experiences. Paul insists that this would merely splice spiri-

---

destructive behaviors such as alcoholism or drug addiction, it is hardly a "trivial observation" that a large gulf frequently separates what we ought to do from what we actually do.

tual experiences into distinctions without any difference. If it is the fruit of Christ's presence, it is a supernatural experience.

On the other hand, there is one supernatural moment that outshines all others as *the* God-experience par excellence. It is a moment, or series of moments. It can be a quiet awakening encompassing weeks or the violent eruption of overwhelming insight. It is that time when the individual is transformed from an unbeliever into a believer by responding to the gospel of Jesus Christ. This is the greatest miracle of all and the most powerful demonstration of Christ's reality. Whatever the specific details of any believer's conversion story, this change from one category of existence into another is the miracle to beat all miracles. Every conversion experience is a divine encounter, a true theophany or divine revelation, where a human being confronts God eye to eye. This is the encounter that transfigures even the most humble anonymous disciple into the spiritual equivalent of Moses on Mount Sinai (Exodus 19; 33–34), of Elijah on Mount Carmel (1 Kings 18), of Isaiah in the heavenly throne room (Isaiah 6), and perhaps even of Jesus on the Mount of Transfiguration (Mark 9). All subsequent spiritual experiences are mere derivatives, outworkings of this new saving relationship. What matters here is not *how* one comes to Christ but *that* one comes to Christ.

Paul also shows us the flip side, perhaps we can call it the dark side, of his experiential apologetic. When the value of one's conversion experience wanes to the point of insignificance, the former believer teeters on the brink of losing contemporaneity with Jesus. Only contemporaries can enjoy the benefits of faith, and only faith makes one a contemporary. No amount of study, research, or historical investigation or reconstruction will forge a direct line of transition from unbelief to faith. Faith always requires a leap because it always exists with some degree of objective uncertainty. Every historical reconstruction inevitably misses some piece of the ancient puzzle surrounding the historical Jesus. There is no scholarship that will ever answer every question completely. Beware all third, fourth, fifth, or umpteenth "questers" (a nickname for those studying the historical Jesus) in your search for this man! Furthermore, each historical reconstruction invariably distorts some aspect of Christ. There is a pull toward softening his offensiveness. "Jesus would never have said that! That could not have happened!" But any effort to eliminate Christ's offensiveness, however sophisticated our methods, finally surrenders to the power of offense and is a rejection of true faith. Faith overcomes offense not by explaining it away but by the passionate embrace of believing nonetheless.

I am convinced that Paul would happily endorse Kierkegaard's insights into New Testament theology. No one ever becomes contemporary with an historical reconstruction of Jesus. Such academic models do not require faith. They are generally constructed in such a way as to diminish the demands of faith, reducing its obstacles so that faith itself becomes reasonable. But saying that one believes in Jesus because a particular reconstruction has made him more plausible, more acceptable, more palatable, more approachable, more understandable is a bit like saying that I have finally come to believe in love because I am now able to measure the serotonin levels of my brain — an argument that will offer very little comfort to my wife and ought not be the verse in any Valentine's Day card.

Jesus approaches the individual, not through historical research and reconstruction, but through hearing the good news of the gospel; fortunately the gospel is robust enough even to shine through academic research. Obeying the gospel's demand to exercise faith in the resurrected Christ allows the believer to see the final revelation of God in the face of our Lord Jesus, making today's believer truly contemporary with the Savior. Historical information may augment the experience of faith, but it can never supplant the necessity of seeing and believing in Christ for oneself.

But, then again, I am only able to recognize this in retrospect.

CHAPTER 5

Believing the Blasphemous Word

Apart from his witness he offers no other proof of his authority. . . .
The object of faith makes itself known only to faith; and this faith is
the only means of access to its object.

R. Bultmann, *The Gospel of John: A Commentary*

A Parable

Two young couples are walking arm-in-arm down a path, one in front of
the other. Both women are talking excitedly to the man at their side, and
both men are nodding their heads and periodically assenting with the appropriate, "Yes . . . I see . . . uh huh."

A fork lies ahead in the pathway and soon the first couple, which has
put some distance between themselves and the other couple following behind, must make a decision: go right or go left? The woman whispers to
her companion, "The trail to the left looks so beautiful," and immediately
both pairs of feet are moving off in that direction.

The second couple now approaches the same fork in the path. They,
too, must make a decision: to the right or to the left? The woman looks in
both directions, and then whispers to the man on her arm, "I am tired and
the path on the right looks like a much easier walk. Let's go that way." The
man nods his head again, as he has done all along, and he promptly turns
to the left following the couple ahead. The young woman, anticipating a

turn to the right finds her arm suddenly jerked away as the two of them walk in opposite directions.

What made the difference? By all appearances both couples were deeply engaged in sharing their confidences: one person was speaking and the other was listening intently. But when it came time to make a mutual decision, reality was shown to be very different from appearance.

Only one man was doing what he seemed to be doing, paying attention to his partner. So when she suggested turning left, they moved in unison. He had obviously been listening all along, so when it came time for them to act together, he heard what she said.

The other man, however, was not paying attention. In fact, his inattention indicated that he probably had stopped listening to his companion some time earlier. Looks can be deceiving: he was nodding his head and grunting quiet affirmations. But he was thoroughly caught up in his own thoughts, not really paying much attention at all. The ruse worked until a moment of decision finally arrived that required him *actually* to be listening. But he was not. Thus the two parted company with a yank.

This physical departure revealed the truth about their relationship. The man's attentions had drifted off some time ago. Perhaps he never listened to anything the woman said. They were now walking in opposite directions, not because the pathway had divided, but because their interests and attention were divided from the beginning.

Faith and Controversy in John

Thus far our study has focused on the nature and the consequences of Christian faith. First, faith has been defined as an impassioned decision, a leap, if you will, to follow Jesus Christ obediently after experiencing his presence in a personal encounter. Second, faith then begins to produce a new understanding of oneself and one's relationship to the world. In fact, so new is this understanding — so discontinuous with our previous way of seeing and understanding — that it could more aptly be called a reinterpretation. Since reinterpretation is a process of transforming prior understandings, the reinterpretation of life must involve the thorough reevaluation of everything that has gone before, good, bad, or indifferent. Perhaps the previously "bad" is now seen to be the good, or maybe longstanding indifference is slowly transformed into the passion.

Faithful Christian living is characterized by such reinterpretations. Both these characteristics of faith, the passionate leap and the thoroughgoing reinterpretation of life, have been highlighted at each stage in this study, whether examining the New Testament's use of the Old Testment, Jesus' ministry in the Synoptic Gospels, or Paul's transformation from Pharisee to apostle.

As we move now to investigate the Gospel of John, each of these components will continue to be developed in John's own unique fashion. In fact, the following related issues are also prominent features of John's portrait of Jesus as the Word of God:

> Jesus' audacious claims to personal authority,
> his disregard for satisfying contemporary expectations,
> his confrontation of the status quo,
> the centrality of both offensiveness and objective uncertainty with regard to faith, and
> the absence of any quantitative, logical bridge linking the before to the after that is created by the leap of faith.

But John also adds his own touch to these themes. For instance, students of John's Gospel have long recognized the importance of legal controversy throughout John's storyline. Jesus is periodically tested and seemingly put on trial by his opponents, the Pharisees and other Jewish leaders.[1] At some points these confrontations take on the official air of a legal contest. The first such controversy appears in John 5:1-47 when Jesus heals a lame man on the Sabbath and then commands him to carry away his own bedding material, both acts being possible breaches of Torah. This initial offense is then paralleled by a second related controversy in 9:1-41, where Jesus heals a blind man on the Sabbath.[2] In both cases an interrogation is initiated by "the Jews" (5:10, 16, 18; 9:18, 22) and/or the Pharisees

---

1. A. E. Harvey, *Jesus on Trial: A Study in the Fourth Gospel* (London: SPCK, 1976); A. T. Lincoln, *Truth on Trial: The Lawsuit Motif in the Fourth Gospel* (Peabody: Hendricksen, 2000); M. Asiedu-Peprah, *Johannine Sabbath Conflicts as Juridical Controversy* (Tübingen: Mohr, 2001); R. E. Brown, *An Introduction to the Gospel of John* (ed. F. J. Maloney; New York: Doubleday, 2003) 69.

2. For different approaches to the clear similarities between these two scenes, see Asiedu-Peprah, *Johannine Sabbath Conflicts*, 24-38; J. L. Martyn, *History and Theology in the Fourth Gospel* (3rd ed.; Louisville: Westminster John Knox, 2003) 72-76.

(9:13, 15, 40).[3] In ch. 5 the leaders interrogate Jesus, while in ch. 9 they question the man who has been healed.[4] In both instances, the interrogation focuses on discovering Jesus' true identity.

Our attention in this chapter will be focused on the first controversy, looking for the various ways in which the ensuing debate crystallizes each of the issues surrounding Jesus' call to faith throughout John's Gospel.

Confronting the Offensive Word

We have seen that the Synoptic Gospels portray Jesus as a self-assured miracle worker who amazes his audiences, sometimes into awed silence (chapter 3). As we come to John's Gospel we similarly find an amazing Jesus, now amplified many times over as the preexistent Logos, who not only amazes but utterly befuddles both friend and foe alike (3:1-10; 4:7-26; 6:60-66; 7:20, 30-36; 8:58-59, and passim). He is the agent of creation become human flesh (1:1-18), the preexistent Word of God who now speaks the very words of God for human ears to hear.[5] In fact, Jesus' words become a new form of prophetic Scripture when his predictions are noted (6:39; 12:32-33) and quoted (18:9) as prophecies destined for fulfillment in his own lifetime (18:32). John also draws attention to additional moments when such retrospective insight occurs for others just as anticipated by Je-

3. Two important Johannine elements are illustrated by this evidence. First, we are introduced to John's tendency to refer to "the Jews" somewhat indefinitely as opponents in general. Note that the usage in John 9 makes clear that "the Jews" under discussion were Pharisees. This observation leads to the second Johannine element: the story functions on two levels simultaneously. On the historical level, John preserves the historic detail of Pharisaic opposition to Jesus. On the reader-narrative level, the generalization from Pharisees to "the Jews" testifies to the struggles of a later period after the church's separation from the synagogue.

4. In this way, both narratives follow the Old Testament *rîb*-pattern of a two-party juridical controversy as opposed to the three-party trial scenario; John 9 eventually produces the guilty verdict (9:22, 34) missing from the conclusion of ch. 5; see P. Bovati, *Re-Establishing Justice: Legal Terms, Concepts and Procedures in the Hebrew Bible* (trans. M. J. Smith; Sheffield: Sheffield Academic, 1994) 30-166; Asiedu-Peprah, *Johannine Sabbath Conflicts*, 11-51.

5. See any of the major commentaries for the development of these themes, e.g., Brown, Bultmann, Carson, or Schnackenburg. For an excellent development of the thematic relationship between the Logos in John's prologue and Jesus' spoken words throughout the Gospel, see R. H. Gundry, *Jesus the Word According to John the Sectarian* (Grand Rapids: Eerdmans, 2002) 1-50.

sus (2:22; 12:16).[6] John 13:7 is axiomatic in this regard: "Jesus replied, 'You do not realize now what I am doing, but later you will understand.'" He explicitly draws attention to the disciples' need for retrospective interpretation if they hope to achieve anything approaching an adequate understanding of Jesus' life or teaching. During Jesus' earthly ministry it is unavoidable that the disciples will follow Jesus forward but only understand him backward. But he is fully aware of the various ways in which his life is simultaneously the fulfillment of prophecy and the prophecy of future fulfillments. He views the world from 70,000 fathoms high. He is able to spontaneously interpret past, present, and future, each in light of the other, because he alone is rooted in eternity even while standing in time and space. Only Jesus can live his life *and* understand it from the same direction at the same time, whether forward, backward, or inside out.

As if these personal claims were not sufficiently offensive, even blasphemous, in the ears of Jesus' contemporaries, he further stirs the ire of his interrogators in John 5, not by urging them to reinterpret their pasts but by doing it for them. He is convinced that by rejecting him and being offended at his personal claims, the leaders have revealed the truth about themselves, both present and past. According to John's Jesus, they have never been devoted to God, despite all appearances to the contrary. His intrusion into their religious debates was not an opportunity for godly men to make a tough decision for or against Jesus. Rather, he was the occasion for the truth to be revealed about self-deceived people. The religious leaders are shown to "walk with God" much as the second man had walked with his female companion in the parable told above. They appeared ever so attentive on the outside, but on the inside they were disinterested, aloof, and disconnected.

Not even Paul's Damascus road experience had led him to such horrific conclusions about his past. Though the heavenly Christ had forced Paul to reconsider his relationship to God, the law, the Scriptures, and the covenantal community, he never repudiated the sincerity of his Pharisaic devotion. The one exception would be his regret over his brief persecution of the Christian church. Paul's zeal did eventually become seriously misguided, but in his mind it was always a genuine passion for the ways of the Lord. Paul's religion needed Christ's revelation in order to be rectified, but

6. For further development of these Johannine dynamics, see A. Reinhartz, "Jesus as Prophet: Predictive Prolepses in the Fourth Gospel," *Journal for the Study of the New Testament* 36 (1989): 3-16.

there is no evidence to suggest that Paul viewed the majority of his life as anything other than true devotion through and through.

The Johannine Jesus, on the other hand, takes faith's work of existential reevaluation to its ultimate degree. By embracing offense and rejecting Jesus, the religious leaders demonstrate that they have never genuinely loved God at all, ever. They have never listened to their walking partner. Consequently, their past "devotion" not only stands in need of redirection but requires wholesale repudiation followed by heartfelt confession and repentance. In commenting on this dynamic in John 5:42, Bultmann aptly observes, "Man's resistance to God, *of which man himself is unaware,* is thrown into relief by the light of the revelation, inasmuch as men reject the claim of the Revealer."[7] In other words, an individual's *present* relationship to Jesus reveals the truth about that person's *past* relationship to God. Taking offense at Christ and refusing faith today is visible proof that I have *always* refused God entrance into my life, no matter how regularly I have prayed, attended church, or studied the Scriptures. In effect, I was only nodding my head and grunting while thinking my own thoughts; I was never truly engaged in relating to Another.

Calling Up the Witnesses

Jesus leads his interrogators to this shocking conclusion by way of the witnesses which he summons to testify on his behalf in that portion of the controversy found in John 5:31-47. Even though Jesus is not strictly on trial, he notes in v. 31 that the Old Testament requires multiple witnesses before anyone is judged guilty of a crime (Deut. 17:6; 19:15; Num. 35:30). So, rather than defend himself, which would be insufficient testimony on its own (but compare John 8:14), Jesus appeals to several witnesses in his defense in this order:

introduction to the Father's testimony (v. 32),[8]
testimony of John the Baptist, offered in deference to the leaders' earlier interest in John (vv. 33-35),[9]

---

7. *The Gospel of John: A Commentary* (trans. G. R. Beasley-Murray et al.; Philadelphia: Westminster, 1971) 270, emphasis added.

8. For the evidence that "the other" referred to is the Father, see R. E. Brown, *The Gospel According to John* (2 vols.; Garden City: Doubleday, 1966) 1:224; Bultmann, *Gospel of John,* 264.

9. For the benefit of his audience, Jesus briefly mentions the testimony of John the Bap-

testimony of Jesus' works, given to him by the Father (v. 36),
testimony of the Father himself (vv. 37-38), and
testimony of the Scriptures, which are given by the Father (vv. 39-40).

To understand the content of this testimony, Jesus points his audience back to the discourse in vv. 19-30, where he initially explained the extraordinary unity that exists between himself and the Father. After being charged with blasphemy for his Sabbath teaching (vv. 16-18), Jesus audaciously responded by presenting himself as the living embodiment of the Father-Creator's purposes for the world (vv. 17, 21-27). It is in his bodily existence that Jesus perfectly executes the Father's plans. These two forever walk arm-in-arm, Jesus always hanging on every word the Father has to say, always responding promptly to any divine intimation, no matter how softly spoken. Thus Jesus only says and does whatever he sees and hears the Father doing and saying (vv. 19-20, 30). The dynamic of the Father's life is Jesus' life, and Jesus' life and the Father's life are in plain sight on history's stage. So Jesus can later shockingly inform Philip, "Anyone who has seen me has seen the Father. . . . Don't you believe that I am in the Father, and that the Father is in me?" (14:9-10). The development of this particular theme and its various outworkings is at the heart of what makes John's Gospel so unique.

Jesus' appeal to these other "independent" witnesses is supremely odd in that they are not truly independent at all. Jesus' appeal actually remains thoroughly self-referential. In other words, Jesus depends on a second set of self-assertions (vv. 31-45) as evidence to validate his earlier self-assertions (vv. 19-30). Jesus essentially insists that his hearers should believe him because he says so! Hardly a winning strategy in most courts of law.

Notice, first, that all three sources of testimony, Jesus' works, the Father, and the Scriptures, are traceable to a single source: the Father. Jesus claims that everything he does (his "works"), whether signs, miracles, teaching, or personal interactions, are all the doings of his heavenly Father. Thus the Father's works in and through Jesus are also the Father's own testimony to Jesus. They represent one and the same thing. There is actually

---

tist since his opponents had once shown an interest in John's preaching (1:21-28). It is clear that this is an act of accommodation on Jesus' part, one final attempt to make a spiritual connection with his accusers (5:33-35). Jesus does not depend on John's testimony in the same way as he does on the Father's and thus claims, "I have testimony weightier than that of John" (v. 36a).

only one witness available on Jesus' behalf, and he is not one to be hauled down from heaven to sit still for anyone's arraignment. At the end of the day, all Jesus really has to offer in his defense is his own insistence that his life's work is the Father's work. Jesus claims that his judgments are the Father's, that he gives eternal life to those who accept him as the Father's representative, and that he has the authority to condemn anyone that rejects him in his capacity as Revealer.

But where is the proof? C. K. Barrett captured the conundrum well:[10]

> The witness of the Father is granted to those who believe in the Son. Those who do not believe in Jesus do not hear the voice of God. . . . The witness of the Father is thus not immediately accessible and assessable; the observer cannot sit in judgement upon it and then decide whether or not he will believe in Jesus. He must believe in Jesus first and then he will receive the direct testimony from God.

In effect, according to John, Jesus insists that *he is his own proof.*[11] Faith in Jesus is self-authenticating, just as offense at Jesus is self-perpetuating. There is no independent outside proof, no logical demonstrable bridge for one to travel across from skepticism to faith. Nothing measurable, tangible, or objectively certain can assure the investigator that Jesus is in fact the eternal Logos sent from God. Neither is there any cure, aside from faith itself, for those who balk at this state of affairs. Faith precedes understanding.

Researching One's Way to Faith?

Up to this point, we have glossed over the third source of testimony mentioned by Jesus: God's word in the Scriptures. Jesus appeals to this final

---

10. *The Gospel According to St. John* (2nd ed.; Philadelphia: Westminster, 1978) 266-67.

11. Bultmann also makes this crucial point eloquently, "[T]he witness which accredits him, i.e. the Father's witness *to* him, and the witness which he *bears* to what he has seen and heard, are identical. Apart from his witness he offers no other proof of his authority which might provide a man with a *means* of believing in that witness. The hearer who asks can be referred only to the very thing whose validity he is questioning, to the object of faith itself. There are no criteria for determining the validity of the claim of the revelation, whether it be the reliable witness of others, or rational or ethical standards, or inner experiences. The object of faith makes itself known only to faith; and this faith is the only means of access to its object" (*Gospel of John*, 266).

witness in order to launch a further condemnation of Pharisaic unbelief (John 5:39-47). This closing section is introduced and concluded[12] by statements that might easily be misunderstood:

> You study the scriptures because you think to find eternal life in them, and they are a witness to me. Yet, you do not wish to come to me to have life. (vv. 39-40)

> For if you believed Moses, you would believe in me, since he wrote about me. . . . But if you do not believe what he wrote, how will you believe the things that I say? (vv. 46-47)

Outside John's context one might easily read these words as saying that correct interpretation of Scripture creates a template that may be used in recognizing and properly identifying the Messiah. Bible study becomes a discipline that equips the diligent student in distinguishing truth from falsehood by describing each in advance. Scripture provides an objective measuring stick that can be held up against anyone who claims to be sent from God. Such claims will, quite rightly, be subject to proper, objective, scriptural scrutiny. When the biblical information is aligned correctly with the Galilean who is stirring messianic expectations, then faith in Jesus becomes the reasonable result.

However, to read these verses in this way is seriously problematic. If this is what Jesus intended to say about the role of Scripture in illuminating his mission, it stands at odds with everything else in the passage. In the Jewish world of Jesus' day as much as today, serious students regularly arrived at different conclusions while searching the same texts. The competing schools and sects of first-century Judaism are testimony to this. It was possible that a sincere student of the Old Testament could hold up a carefully drawn messianic template constructed through a diligent course of study and piously conclude that Jesus was a fraud.

Yet *Jesus never allows for this possibility.* According to John's Gospel, it is impossible to study the Scriptures sincerely and yet fail to recognize the Messiah when he comes. Positing the relationship between Jesus' personal claims and scriptural teaching described above cuts against the grain of ev-

---

12. A compositional device called "inclusio." It is used to draw the reader's attention to a particular theme or issue in the intervening material.

erything else he says about the nature of genuine testimony in John 5. He insists that faith is not the logical result of knowing all the right information; it is first and foremost a particular *way of seeing* that information. Recognizing Jesus as Messiah is not a matter of *what* one sees (whether Jesus fits the right categories); it is a matter of *how* one looks (with or without faith in Jesus). Consequently, Jesus is actually condemning the leaders' entire approach to research. Had they been "looking" appropriately they would have "seen" what they needed to see when encountering Jesus. His witness is self-authenticating even with respect to the testimony of Scripture. The Scriptures do not interpret the meaning of his life; rather his life correctly interprets the meaning of Scripture (see chapter 2 above). Thus objective research in and of itself, Jesus warns, is never sufficient to produce genuine faith, a lesson that our friend Kierkegaard never tired of repeating. It is like waiting for a chimpanzee at the keyboard to produce Shakespeare. It is not going to happen.

As lifelong students of the Hebrew Bible, Jesus' opponents failed to understand, as Kierkegaard would say, that reflection alone never produces faith, that faith is immediacy *after* reflection not immediacy *by* reflection. Faith is an immediacy found by passionately willing oneself to trust in the paradox of Christ, the eternal Word become flesh. Reflection per se, engaging in intellectual activities such as theology, philosophy, or logic, never translates directly into faith. There is no bridge. Apparently, this was one of the religious leaders' great mistakes. They were expecting to discover a direct, quantitative transition from unbelief to faith in the Messiah while carefully following a road map they had drawn during their studies.

However, rather than produce faith, reflection is much better at merely reproducing itself, endlessly at times, in what Kierkegaard referred to as the "endless parenthesis."[13] An endless parenthesis unfolds when ideas are scrutinized for interminable nuance and endless qualification. In endless parenthesis the analysis becomes ever more complex as the idea is held up to the fine light of mental scrutiny and then turned over and over and over again. As Kierkegaard comments, "it can keep on for any length of time and run itself in circles."[14] This process may be appropriate in some disciplines. However, in theology and the religious life, especially

---

13. For a few examples, see *Concluding Unscientific Postscript to* Philosophical Fragments (Princeton: Princeton University Press, 1992) 28, 29, 38, 41, 47.

14. *Concluding Unscientific Postscript,* 335.

when the individual is confronted with Jesus' outrageous claims to be the only Way to Truth and Life (John 14:6), reflection must come to a conclusion, to a personal decision leading to action.

Jesus confronts the Jewish leaders with precisely this moment of decision. It was time for them to make *the leap,* to become *contemporaries* of Christ. But apparently their many debates and textual investigations had not led them to the precipice of faith. They had become victims of their own endless parenthesis. In fact, their research was the greatest obstacle to the birth of faith. Not only did they not see the need to believe, they remained blind to the canyon standing before them waiting to be crossed. In failing to acknowledge Jesus as the Messiah they never anticipated, they proved faithless. Thus Jesus insists that all their fine-tuned learning and erudition has become an insurmountable obstacle to the very possibility of faith. As Bultmann observed:[15]

> Their "searching" in the Scriptures makes them deaf to Jesus' word. . . . The possession of their tradition, on which they base their security, only blinds them to the revelation which confronts them.

The endless parenthesis has struck again! The decisive factor is how they respond to Jesus *right now,* not how they have read the Scriptures or understood its traditions in the past. All those who have genuinely loved Yahweh will now take the necessary leap of faith on *the basis of Jesus' testimony alone* (John 5:46). Those who loved study, reading, and research but never truly loved God will continue to object that Jesus' "proofs" are insufficient and that he fails to meet the biblical qualifications (v. 47).

Learning to Think Subjectively

The central role of academic research in this particular contest between Jesus and his adversaries provides an opportunity to investigate additional nuances in Kierkegaard's analysis of Christian faith. In fact, we have already begun to touch on one of them: What is the relationship, the good or the bad, between faith and academic biblical and theological studies?

Kierkegaard's description of faith as "the leap" has sometimes earned

15. Bultmann, *Gospel of John,* 268, 336.

him condemnation as an irrationalist, someone who opposes the application of reason to religious questions. He supposedly calls people to make a
thoughtless, subjective leap into an irrational void.[16] But this is a complete
misunderstanding of the man from Denmark.[17] Such a charge is a bit like
accusing a film critic of being anti-film. There is nothing contradictory
about a film critic who loves movies, neither does Kierkegaard's critique of
reason's limitations, especially in the realm of religious and theological
thought, make him an enemy of properly applied rationality.

Kierkegaard's educational achievements, the extensiveness of his
personal library, and his prodigious literary output all provide ample
testimony of his hospitality toward reason and sharp, critical thinking.[18]
In fact, at several points, especially in his *Concluding Unscientific Postscript*, he explicitly commends the value of sound scholarship, particularly in the fields of theology and biblical studies.[19] He also condemns
religious leaders who hold themselves above analytical scrutiny as purveyors of "magical" thinking and outright "superstition."[20] But Kierke-

---

16. Evangelical Christianity has been especially subject to this misrepresentation due to
the influential writings of Francis Schaeffer; see *Escape from Reason* (Downers Grove: Inter-
Varsity, 1968) 42-43, 46, 48, 51; *The God Who Is There* (Downers Grove: InterVarsity, 1968) 21-
22, 44; *The Church before the Watching World* (Downers Grove: InterVarsity, 1971) 15, 17, 20;
He Is There and He Is Not Silent (Wheaton: Tyndale, 1972) 99-10; *How Should We Then Live?*
(Old Tappan: Revell, 1976) 163, 174. Unfortunately, Schaeffer makes sweeping generalizations
that do not reflect any interaction with Kierkegaard's actual writings.

17. Kierkegaard passed his theological exams *cum laude* in 1840, eventually completing
the equivalent of a Ph.D. In addition to Danish, he knew Latin, Greek, Hebrew, German, and
French. At the time of his death his library included "at least eighteen Bibles in original languages and translations into Danish and German, seventy-eight biblical commentaries and
lexica, forty-one volumes of patristic writings in original languages and translations, one
hundred twenty-seven books on dogmatics, and over three hundred volumes of miscella-
neous theological works" (B. Dewey, *The New Obedience: Kierkegaard on Imitation of Christ*
[Washington: Corpus, 1968] 201-2).

18. For a discussion of the relationship between reason and faith in Kierkegaard, see
L. P. Pojman, *The Logic of Subjectivity: Kierkegaard's Philosophy of Religion* (University: University of Alabama Press, 1984); C. S. Evans, *Faith beyond Reason: A Kierkegaardian Account*
(Grand Rapids: Eerdmans, 1998). On the personal aspects of Kierkegaard's education and library, see S. Walsh, *Kierkegaard: Thinking Christianly in an Existential Mode* (Oxford: Oxford University Press, 2009) 5-16.

19. *Concluding Unscientific Postscript*, 23-24, 25, 27-28; *A Literary Review* (New York:
Penguin, 2001) 99.

20. *Concluding Unscientific Postscript*, 44.

gaard also soundly condemns religious thinkers who fail to "think subjectively," which I suspect he would identify as the principal issue at stake in John 5:41-47.

The most thorough, extended discussion of the difference between an objective and a subjective thinker appears in Kierkegaard's *Concluding Unscientific Postscript*. According to Kierkegaard, objective thinking investigates a subject in a detached, impersonal manner, abstracting from the details in order to form a general conception of things. Objective thought attempts to understand the concrete abstractly and universally. The discoveries made through objective thinking may rightly remain utterly indifferent to the researcher's own personal life as the investigator maintains the necessary critical distance from the subject at hand. So, for example, the objective thinker might ask, "What did it mean for someone to be the Messiah in first-century Palestine?" In the process of answering that question, the Scriptures and other ancient literature (the concrete in Kierkegaard's analysis) are investigated with a fine-toothed comb in multiple languages and cross-referenced accordingly. The results are collated and the information is synthesized so that a comprehensive conclusion (the abstract) about Jewish messianism is reached. In describing objective thinking, neither Kierkegaard nor I have any intention of minimizing its importance. Scientific discovery can only be the product of such objective, clinical investigation. But in the area of theological and religious investigation, objective thinking should only be a preliminary stage in the total process; it should never be the end that is sought.

Subjective thinkers, on the other hand, refuse to divorce their investigations from ever-present awareness of their own individual existence. Whereas objective thought moves from the concrete to the abstract, subjective thought moves back again in the opposite direction from the abstract to the concrete. The reciprocal interaction is like the respiratory cycle of a living organism, breathing in and breathing out over and over again. The ultimate goal of subjective thinkers is not simply "to know" but "to exist in what is known." This means holding thought and passion together in a constant exchange that Kierkegaard refers to as *intellectual passion*. This is a state of mind that is always sensitive to the points of possible intersection and consequent interaction between the ideas being investigated (the abstract) and one's own personal, existential circumstances (the concrete). In fact, such intellectual passion is preeminent in the subjective thinker because

for an existing person it is impossible to think about existence without becoming passionate. . . . All existence-issues are passionate, because existence, if one becomes conscious of it, involves passion. To
think about them so as to leave out passion is not to think about
them at all, is to forget the point that one is indeed oneself an existing person.[21]

It is the difference between thinking about love as a concept and actually
being in love with another person. Can a true lover ever consider his beloved dispassionately, without a wellspring of personal concern? If he can,
then he probably is not really in love after all. A lover studies what it means
to be in love with intellectual passion since a deeper understanding is always immediately relevant to deepening the love relationship that now defines his life.

Similarly, whenever a subjective thinker does theology there is always
some important ingredient in the individual's life before God at stake. Recall how closely passion is connected with faith: faith is defined as clinging
passionately to the subjective certainty of Christ's enigma, which forever
remains objectively uncertain. With this in mind, we can understand how
and why Kierkegaard insists that religious research must include a process
of subjective appropriation that brings the fruit of its investigations into
relationship with personal faith.[22] Ultimately, the subjective thinker's
greatest task is to understand oneself in the concrete details of one's particular situation. The greatest task of the religiously subjective thinker is to
understand oneself as a person shaped by the passion of faith. The subjective thinker appropriates with intellectual passion the results of one's research in the concrete details of one's life. Thus, for example, a truly subjective thinker never merely asks, "What would it mean for someone to be
the Messiah?" but always pushes beyond to ask further, "What would it
mean, then, *for me* to meet the Messiah? What claims would he make on
my life? Am I fully prepared for that moment? If not, what must I do right
now in order to be ready? Is my relationship with God such that I will be

---

21. *Concluding Unscientific Postscript*, 350-51.

22. "Faith is the objective uncertainty with the repulsion of the absurd, held fast in the
passion of inwardness, which is the relation of inwardness intensified to its highest. This for-
mula fits only the one who has [Christian] faith, no one else, not even a lover, or an enthusiast, or a thinker, but solely and only the one who has faith, who relates himself to the absolute paradox [of Christ]" (*Concluding Unscientific Postscript*, 611).

spiritually prepared?" This is the process of subjective thinking. Thinkers who investigate religious or theological questions while limiting themselves to objective thought are like an astronomer who takes a moonlight walk late at night and falls over a cliff because he was so engrossed in watching the brilliant, full moon that he never thought to look down at his feet, taking advantage of the moonlight to watch where he was going.

Subjective Thinking and Double Reflection

Since the goal of subjective thinking is to exist in the knowledge of what is being thought, a "duplication" of this knowledge is required by *acting* in accordance with the things that have been learned. Kierkegaard calls this "double reflection." It occurs when an investigator moves from (a) objective understanding to (b) subjective understanding, that then leads to (c) *existential understanding*.[23] The word "understanding" here may prove a bit misleading because it is not something achieved in the mind alone. Rather this understanding occurs in the course of real life. Real or existential understanding is achieved when personal experience is shaped according to the results of both objective and subjective thought. Thus existential understanding is not another stage of thinking per se; it is the existential conclusion of the thinking process in the act of living. Now the astronomer not only observes the moon through her telescope but also avoids the drop-offs along the trail's edge because she takes advantage of the moonlight to guide her footsteps.

In this way the researcher's transformed life becomes the "double reflection" or "duplication" of subjective thought. It is reflected afresh and translated into actual personal existence. For instance, after studying the Scriptures and asking oneself, "Am I fully prepared to meet the Messiah? If not, what must I do right now in order to be ready? Is my relationship with God such that I will be spiritually prepared?" the investigator then responds affirmatively by acting in such a way as to be prepared for the Messiah's appearance.

Christianity, and the Judaism that undergirds it, are examples of what Kierkegaard described as an "existence communication." Christian faith

---

23. On existential understanding, see C. S. Evans, *Kierkegaard's* Fragments *and* Postscript: *The Religious Philosophy of Johannes Climacus* (New York: Humanities, 1999) 102.

demands such reduplication, such living out in subjectivity. It requires a transformed manner of personal existence that is only understandable from within. Understanding a religion, whether objectively or subjectively, no matter how comprehensive, will never create the type of experience Kierkegaard is pushing for. Understanding emerges only when a researcher or student becomes convinced of the religion's theological truth to the point that he or she takes whatever step of faith is necessary and so begins to think, see, feel, and behave according to the dictates of the faith. As Kierkegaard would say, there is a world of difference between knowing what Christianity is and knowing what it is to be a Christian.[24]

Reproducing Christian knowledge in the details of one's personal life will lead the believer to an unavoidable quandary. Christian faith demands the passionate embrace of an immovable paradox: the eternal Word become historical flesh in Jesus of Nazareth, the blasphemous Messiah no one expected. Consequently, the Christian life will always be supremely paradoxical.[25] The Christian must proceed through life holding on to a suprarational paradox — some will call it completely irrational — as the centerpiece of everything else in existence. Since there can be no comprehensively logical account for how the man Jesus can share perfect unity with the being of God the Father, it will remain a lifelong paradox for every Christian. Only in eternity will the answer finally become available to us. Thus the possibility of offense circles the Christian life like a ring of vultures patiently waiting for faith's last gasp. The desire for objective certainty may sow its seeds of doubt anywhere at any time.

Research and the Offensive Paradox

There still remains one central dynamic in John 5 waiting to be explained: the religious leaders' ultimate rejection of Jesus' claims to represent the Father perfectly and completely. While Kierkegaard's thoughts on the role of existence communication and subjective thinking may help to shine light on the religious leaders' behavior in John 5, it does not fully account for

24. *Concluding Unscientific Postscript*, 372; for a fuller discussion of Christianity as an existence communication see also 369-81.

25. "Christianity's being an existence communication . . . makes existing paradoxical, which is why it remains the paradox as long as there is existing and only eternity has the explanation" (*Concluding Unscientific Postscript*, 562).

their frontal assault on Jesus in the first half of the story. Apparently they failed to move deliberately from objective to subjective to existential understanding. Maybe these insights from Kierkegaard can help to explain Jesus' retrospective ability to judge their illegitimate way of studying Scripture. But the fact remains that their personal experience with Jesus does not lead them to faith. They reject him and finally condemn him because he remains the Messiah they never expected, the blasphemous Paradox.

Central to John's Gospel is a Kierkegaardian estimation of Jesus' offensiveness as the incarnate God-man. The Sabbath controversy ensues not merely because Jesus broke the Sabbath law but because he believes in his perfect unity with the Father: "He was even calling God his own Father making himself equal with God" (John 5:18). Setting aside the question of whether calling God "Father" necessarily entailed a claim to "equality with God," John makes it clear that the way in which Jesus described his relationship with his Father struck the Jewish leaders as undeniably blasphemous. And, without doubt, that sort of behavior was well beyond the bounds of any scriptural understanding of messianic expectation. On any reading, first-century Judaism was clear that no Messiah could be a blasphemer. No messianic claimant would ever assert that he had entered into this world after eternally sharing in the Father's glory and that his every word and deed were so perfectly in tune with God's every word and deed that he and the Father were One (cf. 5:19-30; 8:28-56; 10:15, 30, 38; 14:9-13; 15:23; 16:3, 15; 17:5, 21).

Even if these leaders had been engaged in subjective thinking, they still would have bumped up against two obstacles: the complete incongruity separating scriptural testimony from the reality confronting them in Jesus and the utter and complete offensiveness of Jesus' teaching. Subjective thinkers are no different from objective thinkers when it comes to dealing with the two behemoths of offense and paradox created by Jesus of Nazareth. The final step of existential appropriation only occurs when Jesus' offensiveness is overcome by willful, passionate inwardness; the new believer embraces Christ and leaps the looming chasm of objective uncertainty created by the apparent absurdity of Christ's claims. The move from subjective thinking to existential understanding always requires the leap!

Now we have returned full circle to the earlier question raised about Kierkegaard's seeming irrationality. For unbelievers who still wrestle with the problems of Christ's paradoxical offensiveness, the adherence to rational comprehension as the measure of religious truth must be abandoned before one is able to move into the experience of faith.[26] At this initial stage, the believer relinquishes the preeminence of reason, allows it to be crucified (so to speak), and comes to "believe *against* the understanding."[27] Clinging to reason's supremacy will make it impossible ever to believe in Christ. Confronting this challenge in one's priorities and perspectives becomes the daily exercise of faith in real life. The potential of renewed offense is ever present. It must be faced again and again and always answered anew. Much as a recovering alcoholic needs to confront honestly the daily possibility of relapse, so the recovering "objective, rational thinker" must reaffirm that the truth of Christ is apprehended by a recurring act of intellectual passion, not objective deduction.

Once faith is born, a crucial shift in perspective occurs. Once a person becomes a believer and stands inside the circle of faith, the perception of faith standing *against* the understanding is seen in retrospect as faith *transcending* the understanding. After crucifixion comes the resurrection where faith and reason are eventually reintroduced, becoming compatriots in a common task. Reason finally comes to its senses, so to speak, and realizes that faith can know things far beyond reason's capacity to understand. Reason now perceives that the person and work of Christ are beyond its comprehension. Faith survives by passionately clinging with subjective certainty to Christ, the God-man who forever casts a long, dark shadow of objective uncertainty across this physical world of weights and measures. There is no doubt that all those who bow down at reason's altar will forever find Christian teaching an absurd conglomeration of illogical, irrational claims. Doctrines such as the incarnation and the Trinity, for starters, cannot be apprehended by logic alone. On the other hand, anyone who has surrendered their reason at the foot of the cross will discover that Christ hands it back again to be used more appropriately and insightfully in the search for truth. Reason remains essential to our humanity, but the passionate leap of faith allows the Christian disciple to see that "as the heavens are higher than the earth, so are [the Lord's] ways higher than your ways and [the Lord's] thoughts than your thoughts" (Isa. 55:9 NIV). No amount of research in itself is sufficient to imprint that lesson on a human heart.

---

26. *Concluding Unscientific Postscript,* 564.
27. *Concluding Unscientific Postscript,* 565, 568-69.

CHAPTER 6

Education, Experience, and Transformation

A pathos-filled transition can be made by anyone if he wills it, because the transition to the infinite, which consists in pathos, takes only courage.

Kierkegaard, *Papers and Journals*

You have only yourself to consider, not me, who, after all, is "without authority," nor others, which would be a distraction.

Kierkegaard, Preface to *For Self-Examination*

In the past few weeks I have been visited by two students, young men in their early twenties, in search of spiritual and academic direction. Both are religion majors who wanted to tell me something of their spiritual pilgrimage. I could hear the emotion well up in the back of their throats as each began to tell me similar stories.

Both had a powerful conversion experience born of a personal encounter with the resurrected Jesus. This experience was nurtured and affirmed in a church environment sympathetic to such events. Their churches not only valued these encounters but encouraged their members to view the entire Christian life in relational terms. They were discipled to anticipate further, similar experiences as the norm for a believer's spiritual health and development. Christian growth was a matter of "walking with

Jesus." They were taught to expect that Christ would regularly provide them with firsthand direction — by prodding, convicting, encouraging, and, at times, even speaking to them.

Then they went to college *and they chose to major in religion.*

After one year of course work in biblical studies and systematic theology, both men found themselves on the verge of a serious spiritual crisis. What they were learning in religion classes seemed to be at loggerheads with their youthful spirituality. Granted, no youth leader had ever discouraged them from studying their faith more rigorously. Equally, no professor had overtly denigrated the value of religious experience, but devotional Bible studies had not prepared them for the scrutinizing analysis of biblical texts now encountered as standard fare in most college courses. And even though religious experience was never explicitly pooh-poohed in class, the academic study of religion made it clear (implicitly, if not explicitly) that the preferred method of developing Christian knowledge, understanding, and faith was by rigorous critical thinking. Prayer, contemplation, and walking with Jesus were completely sidestepped.

For both men, their past spiritual experiences and present course work appeared not only less and less relevant to each other but increasingly antagonistic. Concluding that their academic studies were forcing them to make a choice between reason and faith, one student dropped out of school and the other took a hiatus from religion courses while considering a new major. Now they were seated in my office wondering if I could advise them on the best way to pursue their studies while maintaining a vital spiritual life. In fact, both were wondering if this was even possible.

Is there room in academic theology for the work of the Holy Spirit? Or are there two mutually exclusive approaches to faith: one based on education and reason, another founded on experience and personal encounter?

Initially, it may seem as though we have returned to the illustration in chapter 2 taken from *The Matrix.* For some, higher education and critical studies become the little red pill that begins to dissolve the imaginary fantasy world of experiential religion. A new, solid, rational reality seemingly emerges in which spiritual understanding is rooted in the reasonable conclusions of higher criticism and grammatical-historical exegesis. The vagaries and subjectivity of personal experience fade away as part of the unreal dream world from which we are awakened. However, unlike the world of *The Matrix,* and contrary to the opinion of not a few academics, the existence of these two approaches is not a matter of either-or. It is an irreducible both-and. We are not seeking to exchange illusion for reality but searching for a way that allows these two approaches to coexist. The real question is: How do rational investigation and spiritual experience properly relate to one another?[1]

The Problem of Offense

Kierkegaard argues that the primary complicating factor to a proper balance between reason and the experience of faith is the problem of personal offense. Faith is not only a matter of mental calculation. Time and again the would-be believer must confront obstacles to faith that can only be surmounted by an act of the will. Throughout this book, I have frequently noted and described the dynamics of offense and the related demand for a willful leap of faith made in response to a personal encounter with Jesus Christ. This reality is described again and again throughout the New Testament.

Once we delved into the subject, you might recall that chapter 2 explored the curious ways in which the New Testament interprets the Old Testament. Significantly, the very nature of Jesus' messiahship had never been foreseen by any of the prophets. Neither had Jesus' contemporaries ever anticipated that their Messiah would look and behave as he did. The sharp discontinuity between Jewish messianic expectations and the actual claims of fulfillment made by Jesus and his early followers left a chasm demanding a faith decision that involved a very deliberate leap. Accepting Jesus' claims required a faith that could overcome the offensiveness involved in putting aside a lifetime of religious instruction and anticipation. Such faith expected Jesus' contemporaries to embrace an utterly unanticipated, suffering deliverer. Once this initial, seemingly irrational, leap of faith was made, it was then followed closely by an equally unexpected interpretive leap. This is what enabled reading the Old Testament Scriptures through the new lens of Christian commitment, a commitment to Jesus that allowed creative, unanticipated meanings that would never have been seen otherwise in the ancient texts.

---

1. For one suggested approach to such integration, see M. McDermott, "The Religious Experience of Students as the Starting Point for Teaching Theology," in *New Dimensions in Religious Experience* (ed. G. Devine; New York: Society of St. Paul, 1971) 251-56.

Our study in chapter 3 of the story of the rich man challenged by Jesus to give all his possessions to the poor further illuminated this New Testament perspective on faith. Jesus makes astonishing assumptions about his own authority. Jesus made obedience to his command synonymous with entering the kingdom of God. He required the rich man to ignore a lifetime of social obligations in order to obey a seemingly unreasonable request. In the end, this was something the rich man refused to do. But according to Jesus, absolute obedience to his command, no matter how farfetched, takes priority over relative social or ethical expectations.[2] The rich man is asked to think beyond his cultural norms. He is to risk becoming an individual, a person of faith, answering the call to step outside mundane expectations in order to follow Jesus. Jesus presents no rationale for this demand except whatever impression of legitimacy and personal authority he conveyed to the rich man in their conversation. The logic of the situation is entirely circular. The man is called to obey Jesus' implicit claim to lordship merely on the basis of Jesus' personal presence.

Succeeding generations of Christian believers have faced a different set of challenges than those who encountered the earthly Jesus face to face. Aside from the obvious issue of Jesus' physical absence, significant cultural shifts have altered the nature of the gospel's potential offense for later generations. In chapter 4 we saw how this new dynamic of offense was addressed by the preaching of the apostle Paul. The shift from a Jewish to a largely Gentile audience prompted this converted Pharisee to adjust his proclamation as he followed his call to become the principle missionary to the Gentile world. Most Gentiles had no preconceived notions of what a Jewish Messiah ought to look like. Thus the intellectual obstacles to faith for such Gentile converts were very different from those confronting Jesus' original Jewish audience. Furthermore, Paul's proclamation of the resurrection and ascension entailed an expanded message. He preached Jesus of Nazareth as the Christ or Messiah, but he also preached Jesus as the preexistent Son who had come to earth and taken on human flesh. Jesus was both the Messiah no one expected and the incarnate Son of God. This evolution in the message, for a Greco-Roman mindset, was every bit as of-

---

2. In this way, Jesus' call to the rich man is another instance of Kierkegaard's famous teleological suspension of the ethical described in *Fear and Trembling*. The "ethical" refers to the behavioral norms established by society. They are not to be ignored, but they are always subordinate to the higher, personal claims made on each individual by God.

fensive as the earthly Jesus' message of his unanticipated messiahship had been to his Jewish contemporaries. There remained for Gentile believers a chasm that still could not be bridged by reason alone. Paul's converts and later generations would continue to be confronted with making a willful decision in order to overcome the offensiveness of the gospel. Paul was convinced that every prospective believer really encountered the resurrected Christ when she heard and responded to the good news. This encounter with the living Jesus was re-presented to every individual listening to Paul's message. Paul's Jesus is immediately accessible and available for a personal relationship with anyone willing to risk the venture of faith. In this way, every authentic Christian life testifies to a personal relationship with Jesus, initiated by that opening encounter experienced in and through the gospel proclamation.

Our New Testament survey culminated in an examination of John's Gospel. In John, we discovered that the pivotal role of faith was crucial for the interpretation of Scripture. However, for John faith is also essential for an accurate understanding of one's entire spiritual life, past and present. John's Gospel affirms, like other New Testament voices, that life may be lived forward but can only be understood backward. John makes the presence or absence of faith in Jesus the litmus test for a person's sincerity or falsehood in her search for God. Genuine searchers will eventually trust in Christ. This decision reveals the truth about a person's faith and authentic pursuit of God. The severe message of John 5 insists that a person's refusal to believe in Jesus' claims of a unique relationship with the Father reveals that any previous life of apparent devotion has in fact been a sham. For John, rejecting Christ, even on the basis of scriptural interpretation and authority, only confirms that lack of faith. As Jesus' opponents sought to discredit his claims as nowhere anticipated by the Old Testament, they merely confirmed Jesus' verdict on their refusal to believe. Faith enables a particular way of seeing, a faithful way of reading. Faith creates the capacity to recognize the truth about Christ, whether the message is seen in Scripture or heard in the gospel proclamation. Thus John adds an additional dimension to the historical offensiveness of Jesus' appearance as the Messiah no one expected. John's Jesus pushes beyond the existential offense that confronted the rich man who was expected to accept Jesus' antisocial demands at face value. John insists that our judgment about Jesus today reveals the truth about our spiritual condition yesterday and the day before. Jesus' offensiveness provides a window that reveals the "backward" essence of my forward-leaning life. According to John, there is no such thing as authentic spirituality, at any stage of life, for those who choose to remain offended by the lordship of Jesus.

Both Kierkegaard and the New Testament agree that the possibility of offense is an intrinsic element of the Christian gospel. This offense is unavoidable regardless of time or the circumstances in which a person is confronted with the message of Jesus. Though the offense of Jesus may involve a break with social norms and alienation of family and friends, still these types of concerns are never the key issue at stake. At the heart of the biblical and Kierkegaardian offense is the fact that the gospel remains intractable to reason alone. Certainly, the gospel may at times prove offensive in the mundane sense of being personally abrasive. But that pales in significance before the fact that the gospel will always strike our "common sense" as unreasonable, if not utterly irrational.[3] The intellectual stumbling block may pertain to claims of a messiahship that in no way resemble the messianic expectations of the Jewish people. It may stem from arguments over Old Testament texts making unprecedented, idiosyncratic claims to fulfillment. For others the offense may relate to the gospel portrait of Jesus' authority, which seems to beg the question as to where that authority comes from. For many in the post-Jewish phase of Christian history (which is most of it), the offense may relate to the Pauline assertion that Christ is the eternal God in mortal flesh. Whatever the obstacle may be, at some point human reason must throw up its hands in frustration and admit either that this piece of the gospel message is incoherent or that its truthfulness eludes reason's grasp. This is why the opposite of offense is not comprehension or understanding but faith, just as the opposite of faith is not skepticism or doubt but sin.

Sin, in this case, is the choice to halt at the precipice, to stop short of faith and to remain offended at the gospel. As we have seen, faith always involves a leap insofar as no one ever grasps the gospel of Jesus Christ through his or her own powers of reflection. The opportunity or "the occasion" to believe, as Kierkegaard would say, can only be given by God

3. D. McCracken, *The Scandal of the Gospels: Jesus, Story, and Offense* (New York: Oxford University Press, 1994) offers an interesting discussion of the theme of offense in both Kierkegaard and the New Testament. While the separate treatments of Kierkegaard and relevant New Testament words are helpful, an implicit confusion of the two muddies the waters concerning Kierkegaard's specific intent in speaking of "offense." Not all instances of New Testament "offense" are the same as Kierkegaardian "offense."

through a firsthand encounter. There is no natural transition from unbelief to believing. With Kierkegaard, it is good to remember that "[f]aith is the objective uncertainty with the repulsion of the absurd, held fast in the passion of inwardness."[4] Faith always declares a sharp break with the past in response to Christ's real presence. Faith is the personal, passionate resurrection that occurs after reason's demise, at that moment when a person believes. Only this type of faith, this kind of leap, is able to bridge the gulf separating "the data that are the initial premises of the inferences involved and the conclusions *that they do not entail*."[5]

Does this make the leap of faith, especially faith evoked through religious experience, irrational? The answer to that question depends on one's view of rationality and its proper role in religious understanding.

Combating Imperialism

The problem with human reason, according to both Kierkegaard and the New Testament, is that it is prone to forget its proper place in the scheme of life. Reason is avidly imperialistic, attempting to plant its victory flag over every dimension of thought whether it belongs there or not. Reason typically assumes an objective, analytical, dispassionate, superior posture, lording it over anything that smacks of personal subjectivity, passion, or spiritual experience. It is this presumption that makes reason spiritually problematic. Imperial reason prejudges the subjectivity of faith according to its own misguided and overinflated view of its own supposed objectivity. Uncorrected, such reason reminds me of the father of the bride in the movie *My Big Fat Greek Wedding*. This Greek patriarch insists that anything of cultural significance can be traced back to the classic Greek era of Plato and Aristotle. Constantly seeking to prove the point for anyone patient enough to listen, he rambles on and on about the etymology of randomly chosen words, insisting that every idea eventually can be traced to a Greek origin. So it is with my big, fat imperial reason, insisting as it does that all worthwhile journeys begin and end at reason's front door.

Christian faith is not opposed to reason per se. But there is an inherent

---

4. *Concluding Unscientific Postscript* (Princeton: Princeton University Press, 1992) 611.

5. M. Westphal, *Kierkegaard's Critique of Reason and Society* (University Park: Pennsylvania State University Press, 1991) 91, emphasis added.

Christian critique toward *unbelieving* ways of reasoning, especially as it relates to matters of faith. Faith finds itself at loggerheads with reason devoid of passion, as Kierkegaard would say. When reason is divorced from any commitment to its own relationship to what is known, impersonal reason becomes the problem. Reason's boastful claim to impartial objectivity is actually intellectual pride. However, human reason cannot exempt itself from what Kierkegaard refers to as the labor of inwardness.[6] Inwardness requires the individual to focus concentrated, sustained attention on the enduring priorities and concerns that give substance and distinctiveness to the personality.[7] Without such inwardness it is impossible to cultivate an authentic spiritual life. In fact, it is impossible to become a mature self of any sort. The irony of imperial reason's self-deception is that it is actually highly subjective while curiously devoid of this essential inwardness. The absence of inwardness ensures that unbelieving reason remains blind to its own crippling prejudice. The reason for this is twofold: reason is sinful, and it is finite and socially conditioned.[8]

As an orthodox Lutheran, Kierkegaard fully embraced Martin Luther's insight into the intellectual effects of sin.[9] Fallen reason is now as treasonous against God as either the will or the emotions. More often than not, claims to be intellectually offended at the gospel are actually a subjective masquerade. Willful disobedience dresses itself in the guise of dispassionate objectivity. This is why Kierkegaard often insists that faith must be *against* the understanding or *beyond* reason. He is not claiming that faith is contrary to or incommensurate with sound thinking. Rather, he is reminding us that faith rejects the arrogance of judging God's salvation. Unfortunately, reason, unvarnished and unredeemed, renders such judgment automatically. When a critic of the Christian gospel characterizes it as "an unbelievably bad science fiction story," as a young man once said to me, the problem is not that dispassionate reason has weighed the gospel and found it lacking in rationality. Rather, the critic has made a personal deci-

6. Westphal, *Kierkegaard's Critique*, 121.

7. C. S. Evans, "Kierkegaard and Plantinga on Belief in God: Subjectivity as the Ground of Properly Basic Religious Beliefs," *Faith and Philosophy* 5 (1988): 34.

8. Westphal, *Kierkegaard's Critique*, 105: "Kierkegaard combined a Lutheran understanding of the noetic effects of sin with the essential insights of the sociology of knowledge to produce a theologically grounded critique of the society in which he lived."

9. Kierkegaard's principal treatments of sin can be found in *The Concept of Anxiety* and *The Sickness unto Death*.

sion not to entertain the truth of the gospel as a serious possibility. The theological term for this predisposition is sin, disobedience against God.

Reason's sinfulness clearly reveals itself in the continual proliferation of a particular brand of scholarship — biblical or theological research that accumulates information while never challenging or transforming the learner. This is what Kierkegaard refers to as the endless parenthesis. Knowledge increases but without any commensurate increase in the researcher's self-understanding. The pretense of objectivity never allows the learner to turn toward inwardness and relate himself to the things being learned, despite the fact that all proper knowledge of God must involve a concern for the knower's relationship to what is known. True religious knowledge, as was said earlier, progresses from objective through subjective to existential understanding. First, research accumulates abstract knowledge — the objective. This knowledge is eventually related to human experience in general — the subjective. Finally, such knowledge touches the details of one's personal life — the existential. The irony of reason's rebellion is that, despite claims to detachment and objectivity, refusing the leap of faith is ultimately a personal decision every bit as subjective as existential appropriation of the things being learned. The rational critic will almost certainly object to this characterization, since rationalists insist that their decisions are based on the reasonable consideration of objective evidence. So let's consider how subjective this "objective" argument really is.

Kierkegaard parodies those students who remain stuck at the level of objective understanding. He suggests that the labor involved in analyzing God's word is often actually an effort to defend oneself against it. In constructing endless parentheses, the scholar behaves like a naughty school boy who, knowing that he will soon get a spanking, stuffs napkins down the seat of his pants. Similarly, a researcher can produce page after page of interpretation and analysis only to layer it all as insulation between God's word and himself. Producing scholarship "in the name of earnestness and zeal for the truth," the researcher never comes round to receiving the personal impression that God's word wishes to make on the individual's life. "This is the most cunning way to remove God's word as far as possible from me," observes Kierkegaard.[10] Since this kind of investigation is never finalized or definitive, it becomes an excuse to defer decision or commit-

---

10. *For Self-Examination, Judge for Yourself* (Princeton: Princeton University Press, 1990) 34-35.

ment indefinitely. As the individual stands before God, this type of non-committal posturing can only be judged as rebellion.

Another point to remember about human reason is that it is always limited by its own historical, social, and cultural situation. A few general observations from the field of the sociology of knowledge will be helpful here. Much more could be said, but it would be beyond the scope of this book.[11]

Reason, like the rest of human experience, is bound by the horizons of its particular place in time and space. As Kierkegaard repeatedly emphasizes, it is impossible for anyone to think about anything in any way other than as an "existing individual." That is, no one is able to escape herself, formed as we are by specific histories with certain experiences, prejudices, and limitations. For the student of theology and biblical studies, this means that scholarship is performed within an academic community that has a very specific set of cultural expectations. These expectations are enforced by the unique social pressure that the academic community brings to bear on its members.[12] Academic supervisors, editorial boards, reappointment, tenure, and peer review committees, and colleagues all help to ensure that community norms are stringently maintained. Even though the stated intention of these multiple layers of oversight is to safeguard the quality of scholarly work, such policing activities do far more than maintain professional standards. This oversight also filters the content of "acceptable" academic investigation, judging what kind of subject matter and which methodologies offer permissible topics and tools for study. Graduate school, in particular, creates a powerful experience of socialization. Here, a student's sense of identity becomes interwoven with professional judgments regarding one's competency and facility with the accepted methods of higher criticism. The educational process tends to shape a student's own subjectivity in such a way as to become hostile to the role of experience and by extension the unavoidable paradox of the gospel.

Jon Levenson has ably chronicled the many ways in which the post-Enlightenment scholarly consensus regarding historical criticism serves as

---

11. Although this sort of sociological analysis is found throughout Kierkegaard's writings, the most concentrated discussion appears in *Two Ages: The Age of Revolution and The Present Age* and *A Literary Review*.

12. For an excellent analysis of the insular culture of academia from an experienced insider, see J. Levenson, *The Hebrew Bible, the Old Testament and Historical Criticism: Jews and Christians in Biblical Studies* (Louisville: Westminster John Knox, 1993).

a secular equivalent to religious fundamentalism. He demonstrates that historical criticism tends to subject all things historical to its ever-present critique. Seldom, however, will it ever shine the light of a healthy skepticism on itself. No method, not even a supposedly "critical" one, is able to serve up thoroughly neutral facts devoid of interpretation. Every critical method is itself an established tradition complete with its own presuppositions, expectations, and values.[13] Akin to other "native tribes," the "tribe" of Academia believes that its particular way of doing things is not only the best way but maybe even the only way. Immersed in that tribal atmosphere, the preferred rhythm of academic drum-beating will seem naturally to be the best way to beat a drum.

It goes further. Every method of study also has a predisposition to select for the type of information most agreeable to its particular way of viewing evidence. There is a definite self-selection process involved. Methods of study tend to "see" the data that they are best able to accommodate. It is a bit like something that happens to me every time I buy a car. Having read up on my chosen vehicle, suddenly, I begin to see that particular make and model, and even a chosen shade of paint, wherever I go. I may never have given any attention to this make or model before, but suddenly I see it everywhere. It always feels quite miraculous. I buy a vehicle, and almost immediately everybody else in the world has one just like mine. I guess I'm quite the trend-setter! In other words, we all notice those things that we have been sensitized to see, the things that we already know how to categorize. Biblical and theological researchers are no different than the average car buyer. However, one thing that higher criticism does not know how to assimilate into the collection and organization of religious knowledge is the spiritual experience of the individual. The claim that an individual has had a firsthand encounter with Jesus Christ is completely beyond the horizon of inquiry.

How can such an experience-based claim contribute in an academically acceptable way? For biblical students for example, how can it lead to a deeper exegetical insight into the biblical text?

Reason easily becomes an all too willing partner in this communal process of self-affirmation by helping to defend the academic collective status quo. Ideas, theories, and conclusions are judged to be reasonable or unreasonable depending on whether they confirm the acceptable scholarly

---

13. *The Hebrew Bible*, 116-17, 119.

consensus. What passes as reason invariably advances the assumptions of the established order.[14] In this way, reason serves the purposes of ideology, distinguishing what is acceptable from what is unacceptable according to the guild. Terms such as "reason" and "knowledge" become instruments of control.[15] As Merold Westphal observes, "rationality secretly serves special interests by providing legitimation for the particular society whose acceptance of it enables it to wear the honorific title, Reason."[16] Who doesn't want their research to be affirmed and their status safely secured within the community of their peers? Granted, Groucho Marx may have insisted that he would never join any club willing to admit him into membership, but few of us are that self-effacing. Like most people, I easily succumb to flattery. I would be happy to renew my membership in whatever club repeatedly elects me president and then tells me what a wonderful job I am doing.

Kierkegaard lived in a society governed by a strong state church where the clergy was heavily influenced by post-Enlightenment biblical criticism and Hegelian philosophy. He sounded an early warning against the codependency of Western cultural norms and the kind of erudition that passes muster as rational thinking. Once more, Kierkegaard's problem was not with reason itself but with the hidden agenda governing reason's cooperation in reinforcing the prejudices of the dominant culture. Thus his lifelong emphasis on the religious significance of the individual, as opposed to the crowd or the herd (as he liked to call it), was not so much an attempt to glorify individualism as it was his way of dethroning the sovereignty of collective opinion. Cultures usually attempt to deify themselves, exacting tribute in the way of conformity from each and every member. By "going along to get along" the individual relieves himself of any need to ex-

14. For a contemporary example, see S. Wasserstrom, "The Medium of the Divine," in *Inquiry into Religious Experience in Early Judaism and Christianity* (Experientia 1, ed. F. Flannery et al.; Atlanta: Society of Biblical Literature, 2008): "Our interpretive challenge is not to be absorbed back into the semantic controls of a soothing home-faith-community, who construe the text as scripture or apocalypse, or vision or whatever. . . . I want to confess that it is not for us scholars and teachers to get too close to religious experience" (80, 81). The author's failure to take account of his own professed allegiance to "a soothing home-faith-community" — in his case, the semantic controls of the humanistic academy — is as stark as is his condescension.

15. C. S. Evans, "The Epistemological Significance of Transformative Religious Experiences: A Kierkegaardian Exploration," *Faith and Philosophy* 8 (1991): 190.

16. *Kierkegaard's Critique*, 115.

ercise the labor of inwardness. Instead, external forces of society are allowed to set the terms of decision-making. Such a surrender of personal responsibility can never coexist with authentic Christian faith.

Kierkegaard sought to encourage sufficient independence in the individual believer that she would eagerly pursue a personal relationship with God apart from the intrusive, often discouraging, influence of social pressure and cultural expectations. He was not so naïve as to think that anyone could or should separate herself completely from society's influence. Still, the individual certainly can possess enough inwardness to march deliberately to the beat of a different drum. For any student or academic professing true Christianity, the boogeyman of spiritual experience must be embraced. It is only by admitting one's subjectivity that anyone comes to understand why making the leap of faith is the only "reasonable" thing to do once the Savior calls your name. If the academic guild chooses to stand aloof from this sort of experience, then so much the worse for the gilded herd.

Having a Transformative Experience

An online video that many have seen shows six basketball players in a circle bounce-passing a basketball among themselves. A commentator instructs the viewer to focus carefully on the ball and to count the number of times it is passed between players. I focused my attention like a laser onto the orange basketball and diligently counted the number of passes from one player to another. The video ended, and the commentator then asked whether I had seen the gorilla. "Gorilla, what gorilla?" I had given the video my complete attention, or so I thought. I counted the thirteen bounce-passes, but I had not noticed any gorilla. Surely, I thought, this had to be a joke. As instructed, I watched the video again. Lo and behold, there throughout the entire exercise was a man dressed in a gorilla suit weaving his way in and out between the players as they continued to pass the ball. How in the world had I missed seeing him?

I had not seen the gorilla because I was not looking for it. I was following the leader's instructions and looking very intently for something else altogether. What lessons can be learned from this man in a gorilla outfit?

First, consider the power of suggestion. Had I been told to count the number of passes *and* to look for the gorilla, I may have missed a few passes, but I most certainly would have noticed the man in the ape suit. Following the directions of an authority figure, here but a voice in a recording, assumes that this authority has some measure of power and superior knowledge. Such assumptions can have immense influence over how we appropriate, evaluate, and catalogue information. This is especially the case in a student-teacher relationship. I am regularly amazed and a bit frightened by how readily students will record my every word as if it were gospel (of course, others completely ignore everything I say). For many, following directions comes easily. Frankly, it takes less effort than thinking for oneself, especially when confronted with an area we feel ill-equipped to manage on our own. Rigid adherence to directions can predetermine what we are able to see.

Second, consider the role of context in conditioning us to see the things that are appropriate to a particular setting. In this case, a basketball court is not where most people would expect to see a gorilla on the loose. However, had the basketball players been recognizable members of a local team with a well-known gorilla mascot, or had they been passing the ball in a jungle setting where we know gorillas to be quite common, then we may well have seen the intrusive gorilla when it first appeared.

Last, consider how the way we see things depends on what we are looking for. If the instructions of an authority figure never mentions gorillas, gorillas are foreign to the setting I am investigating, and I am following instructions by concentrating my full attention on something else altogether, then it is not surprising that the gorilla remains invisible to me. In fact, it is highly unlikely that I will see anything other than what I have been instructed to find. As Kierkegaard observes, "What one sees depends on how one sees. This is because all observation is not merely a receiving, a discovery, but also a creation, and to the extent that it is the latter the decisive factor becomes how the observer himself is."[17]

When it comes to evaluating evidence and argumentation, the average academic has been molded into the kind of observer who is predisposed to ignore the contribution of personal experience. Religious encounter becomes the gorilla on the basketball court, its relevance to interpretation and theological insight being either explicitly denied or left unresolved.

---

17. *Edifying Discourses* (Minneapolis: Augsburg, 1943) 1:67, quoted by C. S. Evans, *Søren Kierkegaard's Christian Psychology: Insight for Counseling and Pastoral Care* (Vancouver: Regent College, 1995) 36. I have been unable to locate the passage in the newer Princeton edition.

This is particularly odd given the pride of place afforded to firsthand personal encounter with Christ throughout the New Testament record.[18] One would hope for a greater level of commensality between the emphasis placed on personal encounter in a religion's sacred texts and the spiritual disposition of its practitioners who devote their lives to studying those texts. I recognize of course that I am making a theological judgment here. I have argued that the New Testament portrays a personal experiential relationship with the living Jesus as foundational to Christian discipleship. Whether or not a Bible reader claims to be a disciple, reborn through a personal experience with the resurrected Jesus, ought necessarily to shape the way she reads and understands Scripture. Accepting this particular theological conclusion entails several additional theological ideas. Connecting subjective and existential knowledge to the correct understanding of Scripture follows on the theological verdict regarding the sinfulness of reason. This stance also follows one's theology of biblical inspiration and authority: a particular approach to hermeneutics, the science of interpretation, is also presumed. It should be crystal clear by now that I am passionately arguing that there ought to be a normative, prescriptive connection between the results of biblical interpretation, the theological accounting of those results, and the individual's engagement with the real-life consequences of faith. If my reader is unwilling to consider the legitimacy of that existential movement from research through reflection to personal existence, then it is unlikely that I can marshal any amount of evidence or argument that will prove persuasive. On the other hand, keeping an open mind to what I am suggesting here may allow just enough space for the dawning of something completely new.[19]

Experiencing a one-on-one encounter with the resurrected Jesus can change an individual in such a way that things previously unseen suddenly become apparent. When the gorilla hits you over the head, it cannot

---

18. See L. T. Johnson, *Religious Experience in Earliest Christianity: A Missing Dimension in New Testament Studies* (Minneapolis: Fortress, 1998); L. Hurtado, *Lord Jesus Christ: Devotion to Jesus in Earliest Christianity* (Grand Rapids: Eerdmans, 2003), especially the section on "Religious Experience," 64-78; J. D. G. Dunn, "Religious Experience in the New Testament," in *Between Experience and Interpretation: Engaging the Writings of the New Testament* (ed. M. Foskett and O. Allen, Jr.; Nashville: Abingdon, 2008).

19. For a good example of such open-mindedness thoughtfully evaluated, see W. Abraham, "The Epistemological Significance of the Inner Witness of the Holy Spirit," *Faith and Philosophy* 7 (1990): 434-50.

be ignored any longer. I may choose to shut my eyes, but I cannot honestly say that I do not know there is an ape in the room. Such encounters may become the transformative experiences that move us from unbelief to faith, from ignorance to understanding, from intellectual pride to reasonable humility. This type of experience offers faith as a gift because in the encounter the object of faith makes himself real to us. The encounter demonstrates that making the leap of faith is the most obvious thing to do despite its supposed "unreasonableness." Confessing our guilt and owning up to reason's sinful, distorted bias makes this impossible admission possible. Christ's "irrational" appearance in our lives is the game changer. By taking these steps the believing individual responds to divine revelation. It is only through a revelation of this sort that the believer comes to recognize that imperial reason must be dethroned and put in its proper place.

Thus a religious encounter may lead to a "basic belief" in the truth of Jesus Christ. Though not arrived at by means of historical scholarship, such a belief has every bit as much intellectual legitimacy.[20] All of us believe any number of things that are not objectively certain, and we accept many of those beliefs on the basis of other beliefs. For example, the typical student believes the truthfulness of her high school history lectures, in part because she may trust in the academic qualifications of the teacher. Furthermore, she may believe in the teacher's qualifications because she accepts the trustworthiness of the school's hiring process. Of course, it is possible that she may one day discover that all her beliefs were unwarranted. Were local reporters to uncover a district-wide scandal concerning hiring of unqualified teachers with bogus résumés, her confidence would be shaken. But that still would not stop her from continuing the general habit of believing many things on the basis of other beliefs.

No series of beliefs can appeal to legitimacy through a chain extending into infinity. Eventually, every sequence of belief-based beliefs must come to an end and rest on the foundation of a "properly basic" belief — that is, a belief that does not require appealing to another foundational belief.

---

20. For a philosopher's brief discussion of properly basic beliefs and their relevance to Kierkegaard, see Evans, "Kierkegaard and Plantinga," 25-27. Examining the place for properly basic beliefs in religion has been done most thoroughly by the analytical philosopher A. Plantinga; see *God and Other Minds: A Study of the Rational Justification of Belief in God* (Ithaca: Cornell University Press, 1990); *Warranted Christian Belief* (Oxford: Oxford University Press, 2000).

Kierkegaard implies, and a number of contemporary philosophers agree, that religious experience can generate such basic, foundational beliefs. In the realm of spiritual experience, a properly basic belief is specific, not an abstraction. Strictly speaking, claiming to believe that "God exists" is not a properly basic belief. But saying that "the Holy Spirit is speaking to me," "Christ has forgiven my sins," or "Jesus is leading me in answer to my prayers" are all properly basic beliefs. Thus it is entirely possible for a transformative religious experience to become the legitimate foundation for a basic belief. This is true even though the experience itself may not serve as evidence for the belief in question.[21] So, when I personally experience what I understand to be the presence of the risen Jesus, I may take that moment to mean that "Jesus is raised from the dead" and that "he has forgiven my sins." Even though my experience may never be acceptable to anyone else as valid *evidence* for the resurrection or for my claim that Jesus forgives sin, it does provide a legitimate *grounding* for my basic belief that I live in a personal relationship with a resurrected, forgiving Savior. I have been changed in such a way that I am enabled to make sense of the evidence Christ has made available to me, both experiential and scriptural.

Acknowledging that a transformative, spiritual experience can have a basic role in the acquisition of religious knowledge does not denigrate, nor does it seek to replace, the quest for historical evidence. The two can coexist without difficulty in a symbiotic, mutually helpful relationship. Basic beliefs cannot ignore historical evidence any more than historical research can legitimately ignore the place of basic beliefs. But this acknowledgement ought to challenge every student and researcher to admit that few if any religious beliefs are ever based solely on empirical evidence objectively considered. Everyone's subjectivity, including unconscious choices of the will, plays some role in the evaluation of evidence and the formulation of beliefs. We have already examined how this operates in the academic community. The question ought to be: What kind of subjectivity do I bring to the table? Am I willing to own up to it? Or, as Kierkegaard would ask, Have I embraced the passion of inwardness that dethrones imperial reason and enables me to make the leap marking a new beginning? Will I make this

---

21. For the relationship of basic beliefs to religious experience and their relevance to Kierkegaard, see Evans, "Epistemological Significance of Transformative Religious Experiences," 180-92; *Passionate Reason: Making Sense of Kierkegaard's* Philosophical Fragments (Bloomington: Indiana University Press, 1992) 111-15, 155-60.

passionate leap that overcomes offense, that is discontinuous with the past, and that allows me to understand the truth about where I have come from?[22] This is *the* question for anyone studying the New Testament, be they a professing Christian or a truly open-minded seeker.

Naturally, if my basic beliefs were ever proven false, I would obviously be proven wrong in what I believed. That is always a possibility. Remember that faith never escapes the risk involved in diving in and swimming through depths of 70,000 fathoms. Taking that kind of risk is unavoidable, but neither is it a risk limited to beliefs based on a transformative experience. Historians run a similar risk themselves. Even the novice student studying the history of Christian theology or biblical studies may notice the number of theories and hypothetical reconstructions founded on the supposedly "assured results" of scientific criticism. But just a little reading will also reveal how many of these theories have now gone the way of the dodo. Few things are more predictable than the impermanence of higher-critical theories and the subjective interpretive reconstructions they are used to prop up.[23]

Accepting the intellectual legitimacy of transformative experiences is essential to recognizing the difference between historical reconstruction and becoming a true contemporary of Jesus. As we discovered with Kierkegaard, true contemporaneity does not flow from accurately projecting oneself into another century or reimagining an ancient culture. Reconstructing the "historical Jesus," in whichever of the multiple historical "quests," does not necessarily bring anyone closer to knowing the historical Jesus. Scholars have come up with a wide variety of critically assured and often contradictory portraits of the man from Nazareth — a revolutionary, a pacifist, a Marxist, a capitalist, a social reformer, a radical antinomian, or a strict, law-abiding Jew, to name a few. Problems arise when scholars invest more authority into their favorite reconstructions of Jesus than in the biblical texts that describe him. Creatively reconstructed ancient "communities"

---

22. "Christianity has no room for sadness: salvation or perdition — salvation ahead of it, perdition behind for everyone who turns around, whatever he sees . . . Christianly understood, to look back, even if it is to gaze at the lovely, enchanting landscape of childhood, is perdition." *Concluding Unscientific Postscript,* 602-3.

23. For an excellent and sometimes scathing dissection of this phenomenon in biblical studies and the overwhelming (if largely unconfessed) influence of personal subjectivity in historical scholarship, see Levenson, *Hebrew Bible,* passim, but particularly pp. 10-27, 51-61, and especially 106-26.

are often granted more credence in divining the meaning of Scripture than are the ancient traditions that take the biblical authors at their word. Such scholarly deference to contemporary theorizing merely bows again before the shrine of imperial reason and keeps it seated firmly on the throne under a pretense of dispassionate objectivity.

True beliefs about Jesus need not be based solely on historical evidence. Leaving aside the fact that what passes as evidence may or may not be understood with historical accuracy, it is only hubris to insist that historical scholarship is the only way of arriving at true beliefs about Jesus. Such a claim cannot itself be warranted by historical scholarship.[24] Rather, it is a philosophical precommitment. Certainly historical scholarship is one way to approach the question of Jesus, but it is not the only way. I am arguing that true beliefs about Jesus may indeed be the fruit of a firsthand encounter. The modern believer can be a genuine contemporary of the historical Jesus by means of commitment, faith, and immediacy.

Becoming Jesus' contemporary in the way I am describing may also support a basic belief in the historicity of the New Testament. Rather than judiciously trusting in Jesus on the basis of scholarly evidence for the Gospels' reliability — a dispassionate decision that requires no actual faith at all — this passionate approach can prove foundational. In other words, it is entirely possible that once the individual experiences a one-on-one encounter with Jesus she will no longer wait for more persuasive evidence before trusting the accuracy of Scripture. She can begin to evaluate the New Testament's trustworthiness on the basis of the transformative experience with its Subject, who brought her to faith in the first place.[25] Transformative experiences need not dispense with intellectual curiosity or critical thinking, override academic interests, or turn the believer into a naïve sucker who believes every spiritual story that comes down the popular pipeline. However, such experiences will allow the believing individual to perceive and evaluate academic subjectivity in light of the subjectivity of faith. The believing academic ought to make room at the scholarly table for the insights acquired through faith and transformative experience.[26]

24. C. S. Evans, *The Historical Christ and the Jesus of Faith: The Incarnational Narrative as History* (Oxford: Clarendon, 1996) 326-27; see also Evans, *Passionate Reason*, 156-57.

25. See Evans, "Epistemological Significance of Transformative Religious Experiences," 189.

26. For instance, see McDermott, "Religious Experience," 256: "Theology has much to offer students if it starts with the realm of their experience. One of the greatest needs of the

Reason Resurrected

Christian faith should not be a mental sedative that puts reason to sleep; instead, it should cause reason to be resurrected. As we have seen, Kierkegaard rightly emphasizes that Christian faith crucifies the understanding. In the Christian story, crucifixion is followed by resurrection: death leads to new life. The demise of imperial reason precedes the vigor of a repentant reason, humbled by its encounter with spiritual realities beyond rational apprehension. This transition is the very leap rejected by the rich young man but passionately embraced by the earliest disciples, the apostle Paul, and by every other believer who responds in faith to the gospel proclamation. This transformation of reason also provided the intellectual impetus behind the creativity of early Christian reinterpretation of the Old Testament and the author of the Gospel of John's insistence that the whole of personal existence is grasped only in retrospect through the eyes of faith.

In emphasizing reason's submission to faith, Kierkegaard simultaneously insisted that we "should not for that reason think poorly of the understanding."[27] God created us with critical thinking faculties, but only a resurrected reason properly understands that its ability to understand is limited. This appreciation is itself a considerable advance in understanding. Greater understanding results when the faithful believe "against the understanding," to use Kierkegaard's phrase once more. Understanding the limits of human reason, the person of faith gains an insight that was previously unavailable to reason alone. Reason is educated by Christian faith. The humility required for this education allows reason to become more serviceable to the task of learning, not less so. Chastised and repentant, reason may engage in more productive academic inquiry. It depends on how academic progress is measured. If we measure theological productivity in terms of truthful understanding of Scripture and the things of God, then a chastened reason has the upper hand. If academic productivity, even in theological circles, is measured by creative theorizing under the tutelage of academic advisors, acquisition of advanced degrees, promotion and tenure, growing book sales, professional recognition, and remaining

---

college student today is a forum in which he can freely and honestly articulate his search for the religious experience, for the role of the transcendent in his life. Theology classes could be this forum."

27. *Concluding Unscientific Postscript*, 565.

an acceptable member of the mainstream, then a discipled reason may or may not be a measurable improvement. Wild stallions are awe-inspiring to watch as they gallop unhindered across the western landscape, but they have little to offer an abandoned traveler, thirsty and desperately in need of transportation. However, once a wild horse has been roped and broken to the saddle, it becomes more than a beautiful sight. Only bridled can it offer an exhilarating ride. So it is with human reason, once independent and unwieldy, now repentant and truly useful.

Of course, the skeptic may object that this argument is a sleight of hand that opens the door to believing in nonsense. There is no denying that faith has been used as a patsy for mental laziness and anti-intellectualism, as well as all sorts of religious charlatanism and spiritual tomfoolery. However, there is a world of difference between submitting reason to something patently irrational and chastening reason through the experience of faith. A belief running contrary to all attempts at logical understanding, such as that the earth is flat, is a very different thing from relating oneself by faith to that which is incomprehensible, such as believing that Jesus of Nazareth is the God-man, the Messiah no one expected.[28] True, the rich young man walked away from Jesus sorely disappointed because of a demand that struck him as thoroughly nonsensical. However, it was his refusal to believe that Jesus could command such authority that made this belief appear nonsensical. He was not offended by illogical nonsense, though he may well have argued as much within himself. Rather, he was offended fundamentally by Jesus' implicit claim to be the living doorway into the kingdom of God. Believing nonsense contrary to all reason and believing something that offends our normal, commonsense way of understanding are two very different things.[29] Certainly, it is always possible for faith to be abused as an

---

28. *Concluding Unscientific Postscript*, 568: "The believing Christian both has and uses his understanding, respects the universally human, does not explain someone's not becoming a Christian as a lack of understanding, but believes Christianity against the understanding and here uses the understanding — in order to see to it that he believes against the understanding. Therefore *he cannot believe nonsense against the understanding*, which one might fear, because *the understanding will penetratingly perceive that it is nonsense and hinder him in believing it*, but he uses the understanding so much that *through it he becomes aware of the incomprehensible*, and now, believing, he relates himself to it against the understanding" (emphasis added).

29. For a helpful discussion of this important distinction, see chapter 6 in Evans, *The Historical Christ*, "Is the Incarnation Logically Possible?" 116-36.

excuse for thoughtlessness. Such abuse, however, does not negate the distinction between chastened reason and irrationality.

Many scholars study the Old and the New Testaments as artifacts of an ancient religion. Others read them as witnesses to a living religious tradition. Yet others view the Bible through a lens of theological tradition that grants the texts divine authority to inform, direct, even to dictate the reader's personal decision-making. Certainly, there must be room for the full spectrum of approaches, informed by faith or not. The methods, tools, attitudes, and theological presuppositions informing the diverse, ecumenical (or even secular) world of biblical and theological scholarship are not to be cast aside for a more rigid fundamental stance. But for those who combine a prayer for wisdom with their lexicography and exegesis, shutting out the role of religious experience just will not do. It is impossible to ignore the importance of a firsthand, transformative encounter with Jesus Christ as a centerpiece to all Christian learning and understanding, no matter how simple or erudite. For a believing student or scholar, the New Testament provides the paradigm for what it means to be a Christian in the modern world. Although this claim may sound offensive to some, the problem of offense lies at the heart of the gospel. As Jesus warned his disciples, in one of Kierkegaard's favorite texts, "Blessed is the one who is in no way offended by me" (Matt. 11:6).

Index of Subjects and Names

Index of Scripture References